Barely Afloat

Mostly Adrift

Always Laughing

Barely Afloat
Mostly Adrift
Always Laughing

Emma Culshaw Bell

Published in Great Britain in 2025 by Tributary, an imprint of
Foreshore Publishing Limited
86-90 Paul Street London EC2A 4NE
www.foreshorepublishing.com

Text copyright © Emma Culshaw Bell 2025

All rights reserved. No part of this publication may be reproduced, stored in a retrieval system, or transmitted, in any form or by any means, electronic, mechanical, photocopying, recording or otherwise, without the prior permission of the publisher.

Without in any way limiting the author's and publisher's exclusive rights under copyright, any use of this publication to "train" generative artificial intelligence (AI) technologies to generate text is expressly prohibited. The author reserves all rights to license uses of this work for generative AI training and development of machine learning language models.

Emma Culshaw Bell asserts the moral right to be identified as the author of this work.

ISBN 978-1-0684467-1-9

A CIP catalogue record for this book is available from the British Library

Typeset in Minion Pro

Minion was originally created and released in 1990 by Adobe Systems. Designed by Robert Slimbach, it is inspired by late Renaissance-era type and intended for body text and extended reading. Minion Pro is an update of the original family.

Typeset by Richard Powell
Printed and bound in Great Britain by 4Edge Ltd, Essex.

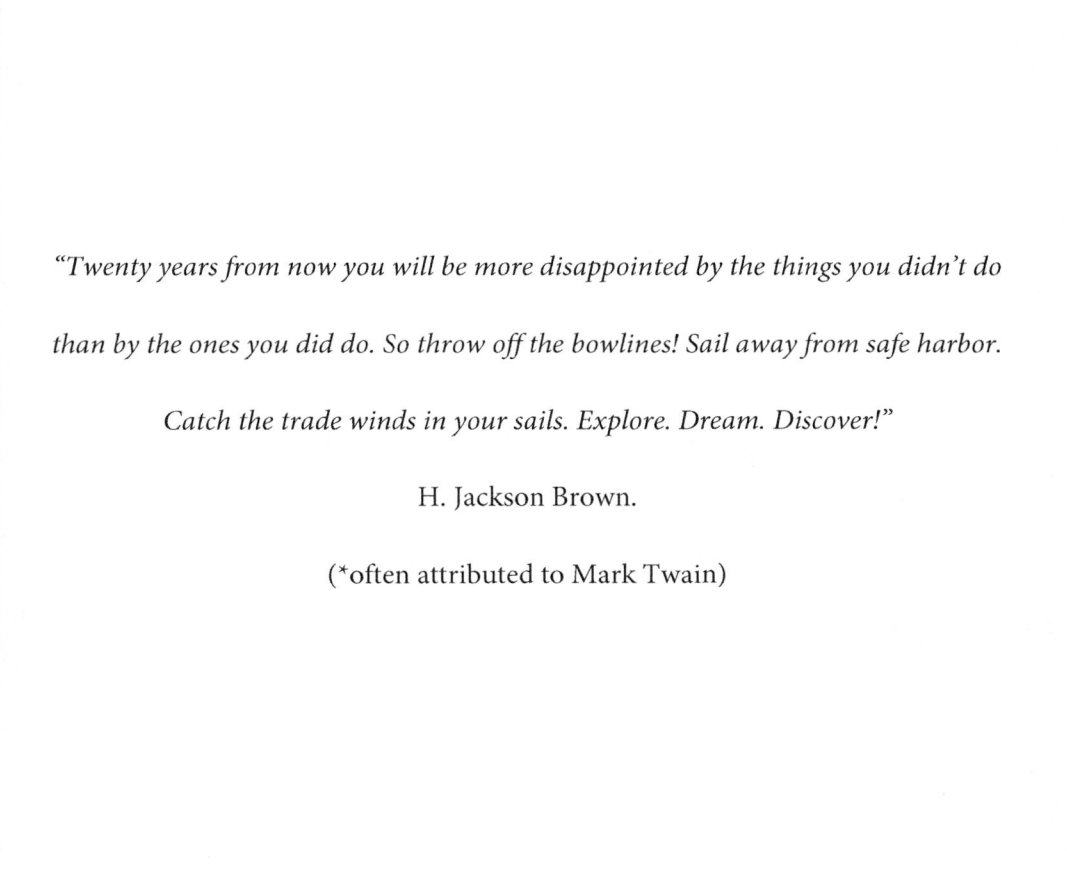

"Twenty years from now you will be more disappointed by the things you didn't do than by the ones you did do. So throw off the bowlines! Sail away from safe harbor. Catch the trade winds in your sails. Explore. Dream. Discover!"

H. Jackson Brown.

(*often attributed to Mark Twain)

PROLOGUE

For Lovers – Jake Fior

Fishing For A Dream – Turin Brakes

Gentle Storm – Elbow

I'm sat here on my little boat moored up and stranded in Litherland, a rough, insalubrious suburb of Liverpool. It's a bit like Scouse Beirut at night with all the street bonfires burning.

It's hoofing down with rain, wind speeds in excess of 40mph. My little adventure of sailing into Liverpool past the Liver buildings and through the inimitable Albert Dock postponed until the weather improves.

I've had to learn a different, c'est la vie approach with this boating affair which is no bad thing for a hot head like me to experience.

Just as well, as well over half of my hair has fallen out due to the prolonged, intense stress and alarming bereavement I have found myself going through over this past year or so.

It's the first of October tomorrow and I have just enough money left in my account to pay for the mortgage and car. After October, that's it. No more money left in the pot.

So why did I do it? And why have I chosen now to tell you about it?

Well. My bone deep, life long friend, Jelly died.

She wasn't supposed to, she was 54 years old.

She was my ear-worm, my confident, my inspiration, my belly laugh.

Now that she has gone, she's left me on this 20' wide canal that feels wider than the Atlantic Ocean and somehow I need to keep navigating this boat and my life without her constant guidance.

I am utterly adrift without her.

You see there wasn't a profound or pivotal moment in my life that she wasn't involved with.

We built our separate creative businesses together, bouncing ideas, suggestions and inspirations off each other. Same went for our romantic relationships, except she was a lot more satirical about my attempts, giving nick names to most of the bedraggled specimens I dragged before her for approval.

It actually got to the point where she said to me 'is there any point in me meeting this one?' Harsh, but true.

I got her back, of course, she wasn't called Jelly for nothing. I always said she had lime green jelly for brains. I could coerce her and trick her into many hilarious situations. Stories abound with that one.

Jel was a bugger though.

When she felt things needed stirring up a bit with my life, when it looked like I needed a kick up the backside, she would chuck grenades in.

In 2015 she WhatsApped me a Mark Twain quote. The 20 years from now one. Do you know it?

"Twenty years from now you will be more disappointed by the things you didn't do than by the ones you did. So throw off the bowlines, sail away from safe harbour, catch the trade winds in your sails".

I'd previously been struggling with my 22 year old marriage for well, nearly 22 years. My two beautiful children were just getting old enough so that I could think of splitting from their dad.

That phrase along with the TV scene where Poldark snogs Demelza for the first time, pushed me over the cliff.

To cut a long and painful story short, I got divorced. However, I will be sniping at that divorce a bit later on, just can't bloody help myself.

Anyway, this new journey all started for me by loading Tinder. Again.

It was lockdown, I'd split up from the loveliest of boyfriends (a relationship obviously too easy for me. I always tend to find a hard way to do things as will become glaringly obvious)

Within hours of obsessive swiping and scrolling I found a strangely exotic man (not what Jelly called him) living on a narrowboat.

I really wasn't sure that this affair was a good idea at all, to be honest. It all seemed a bit scary and unknown, but I decided to sod it and give it a go anyway.

This led to an intense and adventurous love affair with a boat and it's owner and brought out the wild gypsy soul that had been buried deep within me.

I kind of always knew I had a nomad inside me, maybe a tad of a rebel too. I was always off exploring, seeking challenges and this new adventure allowed me to explore the real inner me.

That was the scary bit it turned out, not the narrowboat boyfriend.

Of course I broke the relationship up. It was going far too well. He was getting too close to my tender heart and I couldn't have that now, could I?

Also, Jel really could not stand him, neither could anyone else for that matter.

So she chucked another grenade in.

She gave me a framed lithograph with the phrase "Seek What Sets Your Soul On Fire" printed on it.

That was all it took for me to decide this boat boyfriend was definitely not setting my soul on fire, merely just keeping it warm for a bit.

So that was my tenuous reason for blowing out the narrowboat boyfriend.

In hindsight, I shouldn't really have taken any of her advice.

One year she gave my kids a dead tortoise for Christmas. She thought it was just a slow mover, apparently.

I should have realised her judgement was sometimes a little askew then, I suppose.

What happened after that break up shocked me. I felt like I had lost a limb, the feeling of hollow loss was so profound. Where had this come from?

I thought then that I may have made yet another hot headed mistake.

This happens a lot in my life, but this felt like a biggy.

The blow back from the sense of loss I was feeling had a huge knock on effect.

What I rashly did next, had Jelly reeling and ranting, I can tell you.

Over that year I bought a boat that I didn't know I wanted, spent so much money restoring the bloody thing that I've virtually bankrupt myself and it's seriously looking like I'll have to sell my house to pay for it. The stress of getting so far into the restoration that I couldn't go backwards, just had to plough on, making huge mistakes but also inspirational choices (always aided by Jelly, of course) and the learning curve of all those experiences were enormous. I hadn't even got to the bit where I had to worry about sailing the bloody thing and actually how to achieve it. Never mind how to stop it, moor it, live on it.

In retrospect, maybe I shouldn't have rashly abandoned my career of 35 years to heal my hollow heart by buying a boat. But something had to give, something had to change.

I seemed to always keep repeating the same old stuff, loading Tinder far too often, finding love and carelessly losing it.

It's taken well over a year after this of boat sailing and crashing, adventurous often traumatic navigations involving canals, ships and ditches and of course Jelly's death, for me to finally begin to unpick my tattered heart and soothe my weary soul.

What has truly amazed me about this journey so far is how many people have been so interested in it. Publishers, production companies, television producers and so many other wonderful people. I am simply a woman taking a big risk by following a heart felt path I didn't even know I was on.

Anyway, with the lingering hollowness of this most recent break up, I did a lot of soul searching – mostly via red wine and it began dawning on me that it wasn't the boyfriend I missed, it was actually the boat.

One night soon after this realisation I had a drunken epiphany, (I have a few of these by the way, mainly in the bath) which was to buy a narrowboat.

So that's what I did. Right there and then. I bought a narrowboat. In the bath.

I woke up the next morning, slightly hazy with a feeling that I may have done something rash.

After spending time panic-searching through my phone history, I came across the partially afloat bucket that I'd promised £13k to.

£13k of my own hard earned, self employed money - I've been self employed all my working life, from 18 years old. Never had a job. Unemployable may be a closer definition.

I admitted that boat was financial suicide and managed to wriggle out of the purchase, but the seed had been sown. A narrowboat (and subsequent, subliminal bankruptcy) was now set in my fractured but determined mind.

This all stems from my inherent compulsion to metaphorically kick a table over and flick the 'V's. I cannot sit still and mope. I feel compelled to drive forwards, find a distraction.

I also admit to being addicted to challenges that often seem to include nest building and home making. Addicted to those and a few other things that I probably don't need to mention at the moment.

Looking at it more closely now, in my snug little boat nest, bobbing about in the storm here, I've been searching for a wholeness most of my life. I've always felt incomplete, always desperately searching for that elusive feeling of love.

There may be a reason for that. This is a biggy too, and something I will get to, promise.

But for now, lets get back into the bath, pour a glass of red and continue the story of buying that narrowboat.

CHAPTER 1

DESIGN AND DENIAL

Just to embarrass myself, I have to tell you that music is a huge part of my life (without exception all my friends are extremely scathing about my taste in music, also in my taste in men. but that's another story.)

Nevertheless I still wanted to give you a feel of what I was listening to at particular times in my life and as we're going to end up friends at the end of this, you may as well join the rest of the scathing Philistines.

Fall At Your Feet – Boy and Bear

Scooby Snacks – Fun Lovin' Criminals

Iris – Goo Goo Dolls

I started looking in earnest for a boat. Remarkably it only took a matter of hours before I came across a fantastic example of a rusty old shithole that I was completely sold on.

I asked some boater friends to come take a look. Yep, when I saw it I wanted to buy it. This old dog of a boat smelled proper funky, didn't have the headroom to stand up in and had a raw water engine*

I was allowing my heart to rule my head again (this happens a lot too). My friend talked me out of it (if her husband had tried talking me out of it, I'd have probably bought it. I'm an absolute bugger if men give me a 'no')

Then my carpet fitter (random, I know) came up with an interesting boat that was for sale. It had a

Cruiser stern*. Tick. A Skin tank*. Tick. And was built in 1984, okay.

*Raw water engine. Total fucking nightmare with nothing to be gained and loads to be lost from. The engine sucks water from the canal, cools itself and spits the heated water back out into the canal. Frequently getting blocked with weeds,

constantly overheating because of blockages, and always breaking down. Bloody dreadful design and to be avoided at all costs.

**A cruiser stern is a type of back deck of the boat. There are 3 types. I'll not bore you, but trust me in that this is the fun type of back deck with space for friends to hang out with whilst sailing and partying

***A skin tank is a sealed cooling system that the engine essentially uses water to cool with, returning the heated water to be used domestically. As far as I know.

I took another boater friend along with me to have a look at this one.

This little boat was in dry dock. The engine wouldn't start, the only interior fittings were a giant log burner, a banquet seating arrangement and some freestanding furniture. No bathroom. No hot water. No gas. A decrepit sink was the only attempt at a kitchen.

He categorically stated that I must not buy this boat, it was not good enough. Do not buy it.

So I immediately put £1000 cash down as a deposit.

I had liked her as soon as I saw her anyway, it wasn't just that he had told me 'no', I swear. She was a real cutie and crucially, she was structurally sound.

So on November 12th, 2021, I bought her. The receipt said, "No Warranties, No Guarantees".

Wish I could get away with invoicing like that.

I found a file onboard that day and started reading about her.

Turns out that no, she didn't have a skin tank. Untick. She had a raw water engine. Big untick. She was also considerably older than the sold build date of 1984.

Bastard. Looked like I'd bought a lemon.

It transpired on further investigation that everyone, including myself had missed the big ticks, all the positives.

Dawn Piper, the name of my new acquisition, was built in 1971 by a very well respected boat builder called David Piper. Only the 12th he had built up to then. Still with the immaculate and original single cylinder engine.

Much, much further down the line I was to find out that although the engine was great, everything else was well and truly knackered…that's for later though.

I'd gone and inadvertently fallen in love with a little peach of a boat that was one of the first leisure boats ever built and claimed historic status.

They do say that the boat finds you and I really do believe that in this case.

I hadn't realised at this stage that I really had fallen in love. I'd been so busy looking for a boyfriend it hadn't occurred to me that something so apparently inanimate could begin to fill the gaps in my shredded heart.

Part of the drunken epiphany in the bath crossed with a kind of post pandemic life review had me deciding that designing and refitting the interior of the boat and painting the exterior including sign writing was a genius idea to do by myself. It was also the excuse required to run away from the heart strings that were still tearing at me, not that I realised it then, I was far too far in denial.

Certainly not part of the romantic ideal was the one that had me grafting for 11 hours a day, 6 days a week in sub zero temperatures. That's what it quickly got to, however.

My intention with the boat at the beginning was to rip out only the necessary parts of the interior that had to be remodelled. Jake (daughter Kit's boyfriend) who worked as a local joiner and had a vested interest as he was currently living with Kit and I, and wanted to move onto a narrowboat himself (can't blame him for wanting to move away from his mother in law, surprised he hadn't gone to live in his car, really) He saw this as a good opportunity to learn about refitting a boat without the immediate financial challenge, well, that's what I thought at the beginning, anyway.

We began with absolutely no clue what we were doing. The first thing to go was the spirit level. Bloody pointless on a boat, even out of water. Nothing is straight or level and nothing will remain straight or level once it's in the water.

However, I immediately went completely off piste with the slight remodelling idea and started over enthusiastically ripping out. The giant log burner had to go. That's when the trouble began. A huge hole was cut in the roof for the new flue. More holes were welded, a number of small fires were caused and extinguished.

One particularly alarming welding episode had sparks getting in between the insulation and panelling, it had obviously been checked for fire but that didn't stop me getting up through the night and doing the 1.5 hour round trip to make sure the boat wasn't quietly burning from the inside out.

I was beginning to realise that the massive undertaking which I had made it into, could not be efficiently achieved in the depths of winter on hard standing at the marina where I had bought her.

I had to come up with a cunning plan to refit and paint under cover.

Handily I was working at the time for a client that owned a tractor dealership. I was doing the interior design and full re-style on his farmhouse. (Oh, I forgot to tell you, that's what I do for a living. I'm a decorative artist and designer, which probably makes a bit more sense of why I chose a project -or massive distraction from my heart ache as it's also known as- that included painting and design.)

He had a big tractor depot round the corner from where the boat was in dry dock.

I managed to negotiate (or beg as it's usually known) one of his trailers to load the boat onto, one of his tractors to tow the boat to his depot and one of his lean-to's to keep the boat under to continue the interior refit.

Next was the trickiest part of the erm, negotiation. I needed to bring the boat inside his swanky tractor garage for 5 weeks, taking up an expensive 4 tractor bays to paint the exterior of the boat.

I suggested we could do swops, but he pointed out that he'd already paid me and I'd nearly finished the work for him anyway. Ah.

With the boat now firmly nestled 4m up on his trailer and under his lean-to, work began again. Kind of. Jake pulled out, of course he did. He had realised a lot more quickly than I had that this was a massive undertaking and wanted none of it. Thanks Jake.

I needed to find another cabinet maker, and quickly.

At this point in the story it might be useful for you to imagine my budget as a small manageable sized snowball. Then throw that snowball down Everest. Watch it gain momentum and size to mammoth proportions, reaching the point of no return faster than your bank manager can call a meeting. Because that is exactly what happened.

I did, however, find what transpired to be the perfect cabinet maker for the job. The problem was the cost. Everything that Jake had done (and I'd paid him for) was ripped out with the materials flung in a skip. Back to square one except I was a lot more skint. I snapped pretty quickly after enduring two of the most expensive weeks of my life (3 months at a luxury spa in the Maldives was cheaper, surely?) The new cabinet maker, Gary and I were going to have to have a CHAT.

It was a bit of a bumpy start with Gary. He was great, don't get me wrong. But he couldn't be told which way to do things. It might have helped if I'd known about his absolute obsession with 18mm plywood that he built everything out of. I only had 17' of internal living space! His reasoning for forcing me to agree to using such over sized and over engineered wood was that if the boat sunk, it wouldn't damage his cabinetry. It bloody would sink with that heavy fit out if I couldn't negotiate around his pedantry, that's for sure.

Now, I'm a power crazy and controlling bitch know it all (direct quote from ex husband, that one) so inevitably there were clashes. We soon found our pace though, as I essentially abandoned all hope of negotiating (begging) for any short cuts in labour and materials. Yes, he got his own way with the bloody plywood.

I did keep control of the design though. That really was non negotiable.

I don't think I told you about the boat dimensions, did I?

My little boat is just 30 feet long by the standard narrowboat width of 6'10" and as has previously just been mentioned, only 17 feet of internal living space.

Within that space I required a super-king bed (with Hungarian goose down duvet, let's not get into that spec yet, it will blow your brains out), a full kitchen, log burner for heating, gas boiler for hot water, a sofa pulling out into another double bed and a full bathroom. No bath, obvs, that would be ridiculous. A hot tub was a definite no as well. Just kidding, but it did feel like I was in the realms of fantasy just fitting the basics in.

How was I going to fit it all in?

The bathroom was the linchpin. If I could fit the bathroom in and have a 6' bed, I was confident the rest would fall into place. I had after all designed tiny kitchens before. In fact 5 of my kitchens had patents on them.

I measured and sketched and sketched and measured. I woke in the night with problems and possible solutions. I was bloody demented with it.

All this kept me inevitably distracted from addressing the constant lingering, hollow feeling of loss.

I was still crying in the bath though. Every night. Even Jelly's words of wisdom in the form of 'forget about that boat boyfriend, he was a bullish bellend' couldn't seem to quench the emptiness I was still feeling. However, I powered on during the days. Virtually breaking myself with manual labour and the myriad of peculiar problems in design I had to solve.

There were many other factors I had to contend with as well as the design. The end result had to pass and have a Boat Safety Certificate*

*A bit like an MOT for cars, except this certificate renewable every 4 years was to prove that the boat was safe to live aboard.

Let me just freak you out here about what could happen if the boat wasn't safe. First of all there are the basic flammable components of diesel, gas, electric and coal mostly encased in the wooden-clad interior.

Apart from the obvious smoke, carbon monoxide poisoning, and fire. There's gas. As LPG gas is heavier than air and if you have a leak, it will accumulate in the bottom of the boat and you will not necessarily smell it. The fumes will just sit there until you light your roll up on the back deck after dinner. Then, badoosh!

Another good one is the electrics. It's a well known fact that a lot (I'd go for 90% but then I'm an optimist) of boaters don't know shit about anything but talk like geniuses with regard to working on boats. This fully applies to the electrics on boats. Granted it is a minefield with inverters, 12v, 240v, all those tricky fuse type thingy's and such like. As you can tell I am also a boat genius.

One thing I did realise (when it was pointed out to me, then spelled out to me) was that taking out the main fuse run coming from the batteries and ramming a metal bar across instead is not good. This was the kind of electric 'fix' my little boat had. Apparently it could very easily allow all the internal wires to get so hot that fire would immediately shoot right through the boat and engulf it.

What I haven't told you is this little nugget of horror only came to light by accident, after the full refit, launch and emergency haul out of the water. Here's me wondering why my hair's fallen out.

Anyway. If the layout was going to work and based on all the measuring I'd done, the bathroom would have to be in the middle, the bedroom at the front (bow) and the kitchen and living room at the back (stern).

Pretty simple. Except it wasn't. I made it complicated. And expensive. I over-engineered every aspect (a major part of my life is spent doing this I've since realised).

It wasn't always that way though.

CHAPTER 2

Early Life

This part of my story is very difficult to tell you about. It doesn't come easily as this was a part of my childhood that was hidden from most of my family and friends for many years. However, I told Jelly about it the moment I first met her, a few years later. Some things should never be kept from a person that already felt like your sister within minutes of meeting.

So, like most people, the dysfunction started at an early age. I'll try not to bore you, as we all have our stories.

My mum was a distracted mother. She had a socially busy life and was equally distracted by her antique business. As a result, family life was a complete chaotic mess, obviously unintended but nevertheless it was so.

I was the eldest of 4 with a father somewhat bewildered with the path our family life seemed to have taken. Therefore in essence, there was no one looking after the equilibrium of the family.

I have no idea how, but I felt it my duty to take on the physical and pastoral care of my whole family. Aged 13.

My new, self-appointed role, left me desperate for love and attention (pretty obviously)

I had misguidedly decided that everyone needed the love and attention more than me. So inevitably, it is something I have been left searching for most of my adult life.

The person that gave me the glimmer of the possibility of comfort was my first boyfriend, he was 18 and really should have known better.

I didn't know. I didn't realise. We hadn't even had proper sex but I still ended up pregnant at 14 years of age.

I think we all know that life can catch you out, however, this was a very unexpected catch out for such a young and naïve woman.

Now then, what does a 14 year old do in 1981 when it takes 6 weeks to do a surreptitious pregnancy test in the form of sneaking into a charity shop in the local town for an anonymous test that you get back in 7 days?

It was Neolithic at best in those days. You couldn't get any contraception without the consent of a parent. Couldn't have a pregnancy test without the doctor informing your parents.

So many of my contemporaries at the time were getting back street abortions.

One friend spent all her savings getting an abortion only to end up traumatically poorly from still carrying it's twin. Dreadful.

Another friend (a vegetarian, not that that has any bearing on the story but seems poignant) used abortion as a form of contraception. Equally as dreadful.

These were the times our young selves found ourselves in.

Anyway, before I knew it, I was 12 weeks gone and really had to make a decision on how I was going to get around this problem.

So, this (now 15 year old), with no grounded foundation that makes any sense whatsoever, apart from a moral code that I had no idea existed within me, booked myself into a Catholic convent in Wrexham, North Wales. I am not Catholic, and have no religious beliefs, but this Mother and Baby home within the convent, was the best sanctuary I could find.

Miles away from the only home I knew, I stayed there for 6 months, growing my baby in secret, away from family and friends. My parents knew the truth and supported me, but to everyone else, I was 'away at college'.

That Mother and Baby home was my first dip into gritty real life.

At aged 15 I came across some downright scary females in there, but also some incredibly vulnerable women too. There were monumentally traumatic stories from some women, some really bloody shocking stories as well, with lots of others in between.

One young woman was admitted during my stay (I was the youngest there and was incarcerated the longest) She had massive mental health problems and had been raped. She wasn't even aware she was pregnant until her baby was born a mere 6 days later. Horrific.

Another woman, a regular, it turned out, returned annually to give birth to then give the infant away for adoption days later. Apparently to her, it was a better temporary life than living on the streets.

I remember all those years ago, looking out of the window of my cell in the convent (it was a single room that I had tried my best to nest in with the treasures and trinkets I had brought from my bedroom at home, but still it felt like a cell).

I promised myself that I would make the best, the most beautiful home, the most comfortable nest I could possibly make for my family, for my children. I would turn this trauma around, make a positive from it. I had no doubt in my mind I would achieve that promise I made to myself.

In retrospect that promise may have been part of my long term downfall, yet obtusely my savior as well.

He was born. Eventually, traumatically, after 24 hours of labouring, in an isolated room, with only a bowl of antiseptic, a scalpel, and a nun for the duration. No one else there. No family or friends for support, just a lot of very scary, very pregnant woman shuffling about in slippers along the corridors around me.

Sister Celine the nun that was also my midwife, had a beautiful and pragmatic calling and was such a lovely gentle Irishwoman. She was my rock throughout my whole long stay, as I watched all manner of women with all manner of attitudes, behaviors and addictions pass through the home having their babies swaddled tightly in donated blankets and taken away by other nuns for rehoming god knows where. The mothers never asked, the nuns never said, only that the babies would have better lives away from their birth mothers.

Sister Celine was the one that told me my baby was stuck inside me, in a face up position, and was in danger being starved of oxygen whilst in the birth canal.

She the one that performed the emergency episiotomy. The long cut that allowed my baby to be pulled from me without hospital intervention, in a room, on my own, at just 15 years old in early February 1982.

I named him Adam, first born.

10 days later a social worker came and took him from me. I had opted to give him up for adoption. I knew I couldn't keep him. I did know, however, that I didn't want the nuns to take him. I wanted a formal adoption that could be formally

traced in the future. I was never going to give my baby away without doing my damndest in the future to find him again when the timing was appropriate .

15 years old was not a legal age to be supported by the state. My family was in a free fall with divorce, and dysfunction. I could not, and would not inflict that upbringing upon a child.

Yet, as he left in the arms of that social worker, in his best baby grow and blankets that I had spent all my meagre allowance on, I knew my life would never be the same again. A giant baby shaped hole had opened up in my heart never to be healed.

So I returned home from 'college', pretending nothing had happened, all was well on the outside and internalising my deeply seated grief. I restarted my life at a mere 15 years of age, well, at least I pretended to. I could not restart my broken heart though.

I always hoped I would be reunited with him again. His 18th birthday past, his 21st, 30th. I had no way of knowing if he was dead or alive, my heartbreak continued, perpetually living with the thought of Adam in the back of my mind.

As you can imagine, this has dwelled upon me, affecting every life decision, having an overwhelming bearing on my outlook and lifestyle since.

This is what I was listening to at that traumatic time in my life in 1982.

Come Together In The Morning – Free

Another Brick In The Wall – Pink Floyd

Ticket To The Moon – Electric Light Orchestra

These songs if ever they pop up on the radio or wherever I hear them, immediately transport me back to those months. When they're played, I can smell his hair, his baby powder, feel him for however briefly, in my arms.

And I wonder why I've had trouble ironing my heart out since. Blimey.

CHAPTER 3

THE RUBICS CUBE OF A REFIT

Elusive – Scott Matthews

The Sea – Morcheeba

I Won't Give Up – Jason Mraz

Now, how to fit a full bathroom into a tiny space? The shower could take up the whole of one side of the room and the toilet and sink on the other side, I'd use the middle area for getting changed in and jumping into bed from (the bed took up all the floor space in the bedroom). The first problem was the toilet. How could I access the cassette*, (or the 'briefcase of business' as it's unaffectionately known as) for emptying?

*I'm sure you're all aware of the machinations of a cassette toilet, but just in case, the cassette is the removable receptacle that holds all the wee and poo. It gets taken out and emptied by heroes with bad eyesight and no sense of smell. It's a common misconception I'll have you know that men only fill up a cassette every 2 weeks whereas a woman can fill a cassette up in a matter of hours.

There was no choice but to access the cassette from under the bed. That meant dismantling the bed every time I needed to swop the cassette. Which meant not filling the thing up every few hours. Tricky….

With the toilet and sink positioning sorted, I turned my attention to the shower. I think the design for the shower came from another drunken bath epiphany if I'm honest.

One of the many problems that I faced with the shower was the steeply inclining wall of the cabin. How to waterproof that? I couldn't tile it as the tiles would just fall off, the only solution was to shower board the whole madly shaped cubicle.

But of course I couldn't find any shower board I liked.

I must have an inbuilt motto that says 'why take the easy and cheap route when you can find the most impossibly complicated and expensive route imaginable' which is something that so many people in my life have been frustrated with at one time or another.

I'd had this idea rumbling around in my head ever since my last misguided brainwave. The idea was to find a retro image I liked and reverse print it onto clear polycarbonate board. A hybrid of an idea between the Verre Eglomise* panels that I get commissioned to make for kitchen splash backs and the existing shower panels you get from B&Q.

*Verre Eglomise is an ancient technique that uses reverse painting and gilding on glass. Essentially you end up with a decorative image in front of aged silver or gold leaf, behind glass. I had been trying to design an alternative for splash backs behind cookers in bespoke kitchens rather than the usual tiles or granite and came up with using this technique. There again, the most difficult, complicated and expensive solution imaginable. Strangely enough though, clients love it and it's been a surprising success.

Well I thought this was a pretty obvious idea. Turns out nobody had thought of it. This meant turning a nugget of an idea into a viable solution near bloody impossible.

I turned to Facebook. As any desperado in total denial does. Loads of erudite, friendly and downright piss taking comments later, a magic facebook 'friend' I didn't know I had, popped up with a great solution.

Turns out his company printed signs on polycarbonate for the NHS and had a great team behind him that loved a challenge. Bloody brilliant. Couldn't believe my luck, for once.

That's when the flamingos were born. Fabulous 4 foot tall retro flamingos set in tropical foliage to be printed onto polycarb and used as shower panels. (Bloody gorgeous, who cares about the cost? Something my former husband and I always disagreed on, funnily enough) Only one tricky problem. The shape of the shower cubicle versus the pattern repeat meant that there would be no flow through of image. Specifically, my flamingos would be rendered headless and / or legless. Some computer trickery was needed to fuckabout* with the image.

*For your information fuckabout is an actual word in the Collins dictionary (clearly not the Oxford dictionary, that would be outrageous) I know this for a fact as my Mum's scrabble dictionary always, and I mean always, opened at the fuckabout word page (just glad it wasn't the filching page, urban dictionary. DO NOT look it up)

It was up to Gary to fit out the shower, make the tray and attach the gulper pump* to it.

*I know it's glaringly obvious, but all water drainage holes have to be above the water line. That means using a pump to hoik the water from the shower tray up and out through the elevated skin fitting.

Another problem I had was that the fit was heavy. All fitted in Gary's beloved 18mm ply which made the boat heavier. Which had her sitting lower in the water. As I bought her out of the water with a newly blacked hull, I would only be guessing at the level she would float at.

This was a constant lingering stress to me. Not lessened by the fact that every trade thought it hilarious that I might have underestimated the holes I kept drilling into the side of the hull, having her sink immediately on launch.

At this point I felt like I was personally sinking as well. I was utterly bogged down in the complications of refitting this boat, something I obviously had never done before.

Turning for help anywhere in the boating community I could, only made me more confused and overwhelmed as I now realise everyone, and I mean everyone, has an opinion where boats are concerned.

Comments were mostly well meant, mostly from men, but absolute shite. Why do boaters who have no experience in the areas I was asking about and struggling with, come out with such inane comments?

'You want a gas fitter? I know someone who does electrics.' What the fuck??

'You want help with a plumbing problem? I wouldn't have that fridge, it will drain your batteries.' you get the picture.

Now if you have ever fitted a bathroom out you will appreciate the complications of it. Without exception, something will leak. Times that by 10, throw in a flexing, constantly moving and potentially sinking structure and you can possibly imagine the problems I was having. That and the first 'plumber' I used was a new boater friend (remember my thoughts on boaters' apparent and actual capabilities?). So inevitably, Gary made short work of ripping most of his plumbing out.

Much later I was to find out that Gary's plumbing went behind the tiled hearth with immovable log burner sat on it (what could possibly go wrong with that design?)

One of many water leak traumas and well on into the job, after the kitchen had been fitted, after the log burner had been fitted, I had to get another plumber in. My water pump kept kicking in (a sure sign of a leak if you're not running a tap as it's a pressurised system) He fiddled about a bit under the sink but couldn't find the leak. Next thing, alarmingly the hot water heater fired up simultaneously with an odd hissing noise. Still no sign of a leak. We both started to slightly panic at this stage, something was very obviously wrong. Turns out a connection had blown and the boat was filling up under the floor with lovely warm water. I'd inadvertently got myself an internal paddling pool and a half dismantled boat (again) searching for the bloody leak. Great. Just great.

Anyway, with the bedroom and bathroom layout sorted, I could start designing the kitchen.

The boat was built in 1971 and I wanted to keep the retro styling going within the design.

It was a mad Rubik's Cube of a jigsaw puzzle getting a full kitchen, log burner and sofa bed into 8 x 6 feet of space. And vitally, all looking beautiful.

Also I wanted to have 2 emergency exits. If you were in bed at the front you could exit through the bow doors if you needed to. At the stern, however, if you were on the sofa bed which unfolded widthways across the boat and stopped the main door from opening at the back you were going to be a bit knackered and possibly die a slow and torturous death by fire as you couldn't get out. Probably more valid, if you were socialising on the back deck and the sofa bed was made up, you couldn't easily get in for a wee. The solution was to chop the newly made immaculate door in half. The bottom half staying closed behind the bed, the top half being free to swing open. Ensuring a mad pissed scramble across half a door and a bed to use the loo. Well, there are always sacrifices to be made on a narrowboat it seems.

In fact the whole refit was exactly like a Rubik's Cube, solving one problem just led to more chaos in another area. Alarmingly similar to my life since the divorce. I only knew I could not and would not give in. As I said, alarmingly similar.

However, at this stage it felt like I was rebuilding the boat, whereas my life was still lagging behind and I was still crying in the bath over the isolated enormity of it all.

Jelly, although always there for me, couldn't really help at this practical stage, either. She was well known for being cack handed and impractical. I remember she was ironing once and the steam iron had run out of water. So she unscrewed the back of it and poured water all over the revealed electrics.

So Jel was not a 'go to' for advice, clearly.

But we were on with all of it. It was coming together slowly. Painfully.

CHAPTER 4

EARLY LIFE

I remember things weren't going well at home when I returned home from Wrexham.

Family life was equally chaotic as when I had left it 6 months previously, maybe worse if that was possible. My brothers had gone completely feral, no one really knew where they were or what they got up to, but occasional hair raising reports involving air rifles and BMX bikes permeated through to the rest of us.

Things continued to get even worse and I seemed to be the catalyst for it now that my brothers were off the scene doing god knows what.

I had to bide my time though, for 6 months, to finish my O Levels and get to art college before I could move out.

That was also a tricky time in my life to navigate. Not only had I just given birth in secret and handed my baby over with a strong likelihood of never seeing him again, I also had to turn up at the local secondary school to take my exams, pretending nothing was amiss.

This is somewhere I had never been, as previous to the mad old nun I had home schooling me in the convent, I attended a private girls' school on a bursary. Couldn't go back there, obvs.

Yet another time in my life where I had to brave it out, getting on that school bus in my hippy clothes, no uniform like the rest of the kids, just little heartbroken me, sticking out like a sore thumb.

Some things barely ever change it seems.

I scraped through my exams, applied to numerous art colleges as I wanted to study something slightly off the regular syllabuses. Of course I did! I wanted to study surface pattern design. This proved difficult to achieve, even for me, even with my mum's help ferrying me around to all the art colleges in Lancashire and Greater Manchester. I finally settled, after an aborted stint at a college on the outskirts of Manchester, on going to Southport Art College.

And it was the best thing, apart from having my baby, that I had ever done!

I sunk into that bohemian, artistic life as if it was designed especially for me.

At that point, I knew I had to move out of the family home. Family life was becoming impossible.

The problem was I had no money. I was cleaning the floors at Boots every night after college and working on the sweet trolley* in the local restaurant at the weekends, but it still wasn't enough to afford a bed sit.

The *'sweet trolley' was the height of sophistication in the 80's. The tonnage of Black Forest gateaux I shifted during that time was spectacular. I was promoted onto silver service for a while where I glamorously shovelled Steak Diane (very well done), French Fries (chips), and medley of vegetables (peas and carrots) to guests accompanied by the looped soundtrack of Peter Skellern.

My friend Steph from college was in a similar position, her family life was just dreadful. She worked as an usherette in the local cinema house, back then when you could smoke in them, back when it was a thing to almost have sex on the back row. The sex bit is probably true to this day, I, however, just fall asleep when I go to the pictures. So save your money trying to take me there is today's advice.

Anyway, we knew of a derelict Victorian house near the college and one day went to check it out. It was easy to prise the boarded up door open.

In there, in the boarded up twilight with the stench of damp and rot, we could see potential, albeit desperate potential.

We ended up making our home on the first floor of this house. The ground floor was full of detritus including a whole room full of empty milk bottles (randomly), the second floor was home to caved in roofing slates and bowls to catch the rain.

We ran an extension cable from next door's shed for power. The house still had running water in the surprisingly okay bathroom and we heated water for washing over a camping stove that doubled as a heater. We made a makeshift kitchen on the landing with the most rudimentary utensils and cleaned the place up as much as we could.

I decorated my bedroom with all the precious trinkets I had taken with me to the convent, made a comfortable, pretty little home and lived there happily enough with Steph, our little sanctuary away from the chaos of our family lives for 6 months, until we got kicked out for squatting (next door took exception to the extension cable it seemed) That was my second nest, the first being in that cell in the convent. I was 16 years old.

Rock "N" Roll Fantasy – Bad Company

Rebel Rebel – David Bowie

Roxanne – The Police

CHAPTER 5

LABOUR OF LOVE. KINDA.

Unwind – Guy Garvey

Strict Machine – Goldfrapp

See The World – Gomez

Whilst I was frantically designing and trying to keep ahead of Gary's work, I was also manically repairing, filling, sanding and de-rusting the exterior of the boat. 4 metres up in the depths of winter, under an open ended lean to, which also served as a very effective wind tunnel.

There were no more drunken bath epiphanies to be had at this stage.

This was the bit where I couldn't stop crying. What had I done? I'd created a monster in this restoration and refit and I was literally throwing all my hard earned cash at it.

Being self employed and being that there's only me bringing in the money, I have worked endlessly at building a financial safety net. This started at ground zero after my divorce a mere 7 years previously. The company, with my name on it, that I thought we owned together, apparently we didn't. He did. So that was all the design patents, the commissioned work, all my clients, everything I had worked so hard for gone.

Oh and the block of flats with the rental income we'd bought together which we converted from a disused banking hall. That went too.

I did, however, keep the house. And the mortgage. And the bills.

So what on earth possessed me to spend my whole safety net in such a rash way? I had no idea at that stage (to be honest I still question it now, although I had no idea it would lead to such a profound healing of my soul at that stage either). In fairness though, this was post covid and we all have stories to tell with that one. It had been a conscious decision to change my life and not sit around waiting for something or someone to happen (Back to kicking tables over and flicking the 'V's)

So here I was. If at this point, I snapped something off myself and it stopped me from being able to work and earn money (very likely, I always push too hard and hurt myself) I would be well and truly fucked.

I also ended up with a rash that covered my whole torso. Apparently working in such harsh conditions, grinding the topcoat off the cabin had allowed the dust to penetrate my clothing (god knows how, as I must have had 17 layers on) and react with my skin. It was like the mother ship of shingle rash. Sorry to be so graphic, hope you're not eating. 8 whole weeks of itching, antibiotics and profound loss of humour for me.

After yet more work, the whole exterior was now fully re-welded (more stress as must not burn the tractor dealership down with welding sparks, bloody professional arsonists those welders.)

It took me back to the days when I had started my own business up aged 18 years old. That was an incredibly shitty job too.

There was obviously a pattern to my life which I had been unaware of until now, really. My nests had been built in grim surroundings, yet I made the best of them by grafting and decorating them with my small treasures. The work I found myself doing were the grimmest jobs I could possibly undertake, but the outcome through graft and decoration had the potential to better my life.

Just wait till I tell you about the house I made for my family, a little later on, that was a bloody hard schlep, yet the rewards to all these hardships have been tremendous.

It was now time to take the windows out and get them restored as they were the beautiful original chrome ones.

Now I restore the interiors of historical buildings as part of my specialist paint work job. It seemed obvious to me that there would be a restorer of boat windows handy. Restoration of windows is a thing, isn't it?

Nope. I tried everywhere, everyone. I eventually turned to Facebook again. I'd had one great success before with it, so what was there to lose? Actually, don't answer that.

The offers of help I now got were from boaters. A fundamental difference to my last Facebook request. I now had a near army of 'clued up' boaters that could help.

Hoorah! Except they didn't. Or couldn't. One by one they dropped away. Too big a job for them, or too busy to commit. Bloody boaters.

So I thought, bugger it. I'll do it myself. And I tried, god I tried. I couldn't even get the windows out. They were stuck in so tight that they had to be multi-tooled* out. (How can windows that are fixed in so well, leak so much? It's one of boating life's great conundrums)

*a multi-tool is the 'go to' tool for any tricky job. Need a hole cut in the floor under the sink to access the leaky pipes that the new kitchen has been fitted over? Get the multi-tool on it. Trying to find the electrics that your boat mate has hidden behind the panelling? Multi-tool a lot of holes in the newly finished panelling, that'll do it.

An old friend couldn't bear my moaning any longer and stepped in to help. Phew. The relief was palpable. I virtually threw the removed windows at him and left him with it.

At that point I'd been valiantly soldiering on under the lean to / wind tunnel, up tower scaffolding that I dragged around with me like a recalcitrant child. Gary was also struggling with the conditions and his 'bad feet', bless him.

There was a giant step ladder strapped to the side of the trailer on which the boat sat. Every cut, every 'offer up'* of every cut had to be hoiked up and down the ladder, over the back deck and right through the boat.

*'offer up' is a fine Lancashire term for trying something in position to see if it fits or works.

It was an inefficient and expensive way of working. The boat desperately needed to be in that cosy, heated and swanky tractor garage.

CHAPTER 6

Early Life

After being kicked out of the squat at 16, I went in search of slightly more salubrious accommodation. This took the form of another Victorian house that had previously been converted into bedsits. The word on the street was that the landlord had gone bankrupt and no one had paid rent for months, so you could wing it and live there rent free. The only thing you had to pay for was electricity in the form of a 50p accepting meter.

It was a shithole, of course it was. But it had potential. I borrowed some money from one of the lads at college until my grant came through and decorated my tiny bedsit in the top corner of a house that felt like it was straight out of the Wild West as the other 'tenants' were volatile and mental at best.

I painted it lime green - Peridot. I even remember the name of the colour I bought! (In retrospect, this was obviously the nucleus of my future profession). I was gifted a bed, carpet pieces that I patched together, and got out my camping stove and precious treasures* once again.

*My treasures took the form of small collections I'd picked up at antique markets, my parent's ceramic bride and groom from their wedding cake, 'Whimsies' my grandma had given me. My precious tape recorder with all the self recorded tapes of top 40 hits spliced together in an attempt to omit Terry Vance's voice. My one record, Pink Floyd's 'The Wall'. No record player though.

A collective mixture of the child I had been, the woman I was to become, and the soundtrack to accompany it, I suppose. All kept in a leather suitcase held closed with an old belt. That suitcase got dragged everywhere.

A good 4 months passed before I got broken into. I'd gone home like I always did at the weekend, to serve gateaux to the Lancashire glitterati*.

Monday morning on my return saw the door smashed in and the electricity meter robbed, full of all my 50 pence pieces. It was the other squatters in the house that had done it, the bastards. It unnerved me. I felt unprotected, it hadn't mattered where I made my homes so far, because I had felt they were my sanctuaries, my own personal spaces. Now that had been breached. There was a gaping, splintered hole in my door, the lock had been smashed off and a crow bar had ripped the meter from the wall. I had only just turned 17. Time to move on yet again, I couldn't stay there any longer.

So the old leather suitcase came out yet again and I packed it up, not knowing where the next path would take me.

*The Lancashire glitterati were mainly farmers who grafted hard all day and dressed up as if for a wedding at night. My friend's mum who owned a dairy farm used to come downstairs ready for dinner (dinner in her own home) dressed in a full cocktail dress and clip clop heels. After her pie and chips she'd settle down on the sofa with Sobranie cigarettes kept in an onyx box to watch Dallas and drink Cinzano and lemonade.

I'm delighted to say, she's still alive today and still as glamorous as ever.

Comfortably Numb – Pink Floyd

Waiting For a Girl like you – Foreigner

Every Breath You Take – Police

CHAPTER 7

BOAT FRENZY

Black Star Dancing – High Flying Birds

Circles – JJ Grey and Mofro

Eye For an Eye – UNKLE

Finally on 5th February 2022, after 3 weeks of waiting and working in a wind tunnel, my little boat was towed into the garage. Her home for an absolute maximum of 5 weeks.

My already depleted (I'd lost 12lbs at this point) and rash covered body (don't picture it, you may never recover) ramped into overdrive. I had to get the whole of the exterior of the boat fully painted and sign written, and very importantly watertight. Which also meant hurrying those windows along.

At this point I was working 11 hours a day, 6 days a week. The lads in the garage thankfully were brilliant. Any problems I encountered (several a day) were met with inventive and capable solutions. Alan in particular, a master with a grinder, welding torch and swear word will be forever on my Christmas card list.

We were belting on with the rewiring, plumbing, gas, fitting and painting. I was also spending my evenings researching and purchasing all the weird bits of kit I didn't know existed before. Most of it a gamble that would hopefully be a solution to another boat fitting conundrum.

In another life I'm going to design the correct connections for plumbing, 12 volt wiring and all the other minutiae needed to retro fit a boat out more easily. Give some other bugger a smoother ride than mine had been from the off.

Simultaneously to all this and instigated by my mother (thanks Mum), I decided to get that money pit of a house earning it's keep by putting it on Airbnb. I intended to live on the boat as much as possible, especially in summer (that's the beauty of self employment and trying to not giving a fuck at this stage of my life)

Sounds really straightforward doesn't it? Except I had lived in that house, bringing up my children there for over 20 years. That's 20 years worth of accumulated shite in every cupboard and every drawer and I was only moving out when guests were in. So what to do with all my stuff? What to do with the rammed freezer full of food?

It was too overwhelming. I decided to put the house live on Airbnb with a future start and bookable date of August, six months from then. Except I buggered the schedule up. The first guests immediately booked automatically through Airbnb for April 8th. Fuuuuck.

The second guests to (provisionally) booked you guessed it, also for April, were a pair of motorcycling celebrity chefs. Or rather their production company booked it.

My stress levels and blood pressure cogged up yet another gear. Especially as I could not divert any of my time whatsoever to the conversion of the family home into a viable 5 star rental.

I had to keep going with the work on the boat whilst she was garaged. No choice.

5 weeks of a full time fitter. 5 weeks of me painting 6 coats on everything. Signwriting. Pinstriping.

One of my specialties is colour. I'm actually a colour consultant and I often hand mix bespoke colours, which is what I was going to have to do for my little boat.

I had decided to go for a retro slant on the traditional narrowboat colours of green and red.

Acid lime green for the hull - back to lime green again. Every home I have ever lived in has had a lime green room in some form or other which stems from the green of my Wild West bedsit. In fact the sitting room at home here is called the Green Room, although it's now pink - don't try and reason with that one (Just be glad you're not married to me) and red-orange for the bow and stern elevations, kicking it up with a cobalt blue accent for the pram cover* canvas, piped in the same red-orange.

Just bloody gorgeous.

*A pram cover is the universally accepted colloquial term for the back deck canopy that allows for cruising the cut (get me, sounding like a seasoned boater, I mean sailing down the canal, of course) whilst simultaneously partying out of the rain. Out of interest, the front deck canopy is called the cratch cover. Which to me just sounds wrong, is cripplingly impossible to sit comfortably in and not nearly as much fun.

Now to design the signwriting. Erf. Tricky. Nothing I had seen on any other boat gave me inspiration that would complement my colour scheme and indeed the 50 year old style of the build of the boat. I had to go back to what inspired me in art and design within that 1970's time frame.

I reckon as a rule of thumb, you should always go back to what inspires you anyway. That way you stay true to your own particular style.

I got it down to the Adidas pinstripe (I ended up using 2 stripes and not 3, but let's not split hairs) and the fabulous BIBA font (man alive, Barbara Hulanicki the founder of BIBA, what a woman) for the lettering.

So that was the exterior pretty much bagged.

Now onto the windows.

The bloody 50 year old windows were proving a total nightmare. The seals needed to be replaced. In parallelogram shaped windows. We had to source and adapt rubber seals to fit. It would be a miracle if these didn't leak.

The windows were eventually fitted on the last afternoon of the last day of the fifth week. In a panic. No pressure there then.

Later, when the boat was booked for launch and at the very last minute because of logistics, the boat was towed* into the garage's back yard for seal testing. 6 out of 8 windows leaked profoundly. As did the log burner flue and 2 of the 3 new mushroom roof vents. Talk about going downhill faster than a toboggan.

The launch date was promptly postponed and another window restorer desperately searched for.

*To tow the boat anywhere involved begging one of the busy lads out of the garage to borrow a tractor and tow her out of the garage, down the road and round the corner to the rear yard. All on my client's payroll. I didn't bother the client with this information, obviously. To be fair, he wouldn't have minded. I think he'd got to the same point with me as I had with Gary. Some fights just weren't worth the effort. You'd lose anyway. Poor bugger.

I did eventually find a window restorer. A caravan fitter. Genius! Why didn't I think of using caravan lads before? So Martin came to my rescue. His solution was to fix the windows into the holes using baby shit. Yes. Really. Obviously no babies were actually farmed for their by-product. It was actually a non setting adhesive known in the trade as baby shit. I was even willing to take on real baby shit if it worked at this point. He got to work by taking all the windows out for a second time, yes, a second time, re-sealing them and glueing them back in. With baby shit. Of which I got addicted to (I'm sure you're aware at this point I have quite an addictive personality) I used it to bog and gunk (technical terms for filling holes and gaps) every leaky bit of boat I could find, and believe me, there were many.

My 5 precious weeks were up. The boat was expeditiously dragged out of the swanky garage (phew) and shoved back in the wind tunnel.

Where she was unceremoniously abandoned by all the trades who were desperate to get on with other work. Including me. I had the next shit show lined up in the form of getting the house, studio and goats (Oh my bloody free roaming Pygmy goats. Total escape artists, consumers of everything they're not allowed to, car climbers and utter little bastards) all Airbnb ready.

CHAPTER 8

Early Life

At the low point of the bed sit break in, feeling so vulnerable, with nowhere to go but back home to another type of Wild West, I fell in love. It came out of nowhere. I had tried to be in love before with the father of Adam, but it didn't work. I was too young and traumatised to manage any love bar the love I felt for my baby. I had a lot of growing to do and art college was certainly helping me to get there.

I had always wanted to be in love (I still yearn after love, I seem to find it then carelessly misplace it somewhere), especially after having given my 10 day old baby up for adoption, it had left such a scar on my heart that I thought / hoped love would heal it.

He was a lad from the Art College I was attending, he seemed so much older and cooler and sexier than the other lads there. To add to this sex appeal, he had a motorbike!

We decided to load the bike up and go camping around Cornwall all summer. Besides, we didn't really have anywhere to live at that point in time, anyway.

This was exactly the sort of thing I had imagined my new life and love to be doing. We should have had a guitar strapped to the bike to really finish the whole romantic ideal off for me.

So once again, I had my treasures packed up and thankfully left the Wild West bedsit for good.

Of course we had a great summer. What wasn't to love? Friends came and joined us, we basked on the beautiful rocky beaches, made fires, listened to hippy music.

This was a period of my life that I could open my eyes and heart and embrace my creative side. The patterns in those rocks! The texture of the sea rolling over the sand. The colours! It all needed sketching. Scribbling away in my sketchbook in between laughing, making love and smoking weed.

Of course we fell in love with Cornwall. We fell in love with the whole vibe.

He had been accepted on a fine art degree course at a uni there and he'd found a cottage to rent.

I had begun my second year at Southport Art College and hadn't the qualifications to begin uni, but I couldn't bear the thought of being separated from the love I had craved and found.

I then made probably the biggest mistake of my life and the only mistake I still regret to this day.

I left my beloved Art College. To go and live in Cornwall with my boyfriend. That's how strong the draw was to keep this love in my heart.

The college got onto to me pretty much straight away. My lecturers were aghast that I had done something so rash when I had such potential. I had no idea they had such faith in me.

The grant that I'd taken from them and used to decorate the bedsit needed to be returned (weird how even at this young age I was willing to overspend on interior decoration.)

I was a bit buggered with this repayment as obviously I didn't have it.

Eventually after 10 months of living in Cornwall with the dream life and vibe slightly waning, I had to return home to make the money to repay the grant.

It was kind of time anyway. I realised I needed purpose to sustain me as well as love. That's stayed with me all this time too. You can't just roll around doing little apart from living off love now, can you?

Well, I knew that that I couldn't, at least.

Sweet Dreams – Eurythmics

Something in the Way She Moves – James Taylor

Shooting Star – Bad Company

CHAPTER 9

LOSING MY SHIT

Feeling Oblivion – Turin Brakes

Fire And Rain – James Taylor

My Friend – Groove Armada

I had 3 weeks to turn the house round and also to turn my life upside down. The latter was far too easily achievable, the former a lot more complicated and time consuming.

If you take a look around your own home and look at it through an excited holiday maker's eyes whose life is going to be transformed for a magical family holiday by staying in it. Would it pass muster?

Now open a drawer, clear it out and find a space for all that crap that you have been accumulating for years. It's not like moving house, because you're only temporarily moving out. You can box everything but you are going to need some of that stuff handy sometime soon. So where the hell to put everything?

Now let them shag in your bed.

Are you feeling my pain yet?

I'd decided that if this Airbnb lark was going to be worth my while I had better make it the most luxurious, the most desirable farmhouse imaginable. Sleeping 10 with a stretch of ingenuity and imagination in order to maximise return.

I began in earnest with redecorating, carpeting*, upgrading the bathrooms and emptying my life into boxes. I threw out all my clothes. They didn't fit me anymore anyway as I'd lost over 20lbs in weight. I removed every trace of personal effects like photos, paintings, Netflix login details (that and wiping the 6 Firesticks I had in the house pushed me right over the humour cliff)

It was at this point I realised that I'd also thrown out vital stuff too. That was me going through the bins yet again, including one panicked trip to the dump to recover a notebook of passwords.

*It was a kind of divine retribution for me having my carpet fitter at the house, as it was his fault I got the boat in the first place. Sort of. The goats hadn't been fully contained at this point (it took about another £5k of trying to keep them in, in the end) and they really took to Brian and the contents of his van.

In particular eating great chunks out of the underlay he had in there and dragging out the gripper rods and box, in order to eat the cardboard. They do love cardboard, bless 'em.

As Brian's tidying his van up, the goats get in the house and start doing the wall of death around the kitchen with Brian in hot pursuit. Took him 20 minutes to catch them. It's a memory I will cherish for years to come and will always fall back on if I need cheering up.

One particular low point started with the smallest of problems. My ensuite bath's freestanding mixer tap was leaking. No problem, an easy repair, just a washer. Except it turns out my former husband must have bought the tap from the Chinese slave trade as no washer had ever been in existence since. Trust me. Even my beloved plumber / tiler Ian, couldn't fix it.

I had to buy a new set of taps. Okay. Except the bath had to come out to get to the taps. Okay. So the bath comes out and fuck me there is a massive leak from the waste underneath the bath that was freestanding on the large, carpeted bathroom floor, now with a large black stain on it. So that's the carpet that needs replacing too, if I can beg the carpet fitter to come back that is. Okay, back to replacing the taps. Turns out the original taps had been bolted to a large metal plate that had been bolted to the underside of the floor joists before even the floor had been laid. Slight overkill in my opinion and utterly impossible to get out. The joists had to be cut to get to the plate to get to the taps. Except the iron plate had also been built into the 2' thick farmhouse gable end that I had dropped when renovating in order to get some fancy arrow slot windows in. Days of labour and muttered swear words from the unflappable Ian later, he gets the taps out and begins to back fill the cavernous hole he had to make in order to do it. The new taps go on with a struggle because of the back fill problems. The new carpet gets fitted. Then the simple task of the bath that just needs to be plonked back on the carpet after it's leaky waste is replaced.

Except, my former husband must have bought the bath and integral waste from the Chinese underworld as no other waste would fit the bath. So that's the bath that would have to be replaced too.

Hang on. There's a problem. The bath was craned into the 3rd floor bathroom through the roof of the farmhouse that had been taken off to re slate when I was renovating, because there was no way to get a bath up the 2 flights of twisty 400 year old stairs otherwise.

That was it, that did it. I reached breaking point. A total and profound meltdown ensued. Witnessed by an alarmed Ian. Tears and snot poured out of me and dribbled down me. A full hysterical rant on how I totally give up, sick of being brave doing it on my own, what did I think I was trying to achieve by all of this anyway, think I'll burn it down and move to Ukraine, you know the kind of thing.

Ian quietly went out to his van (which the goats were standing on) got a roll of duct tape and a roll of PTFE tape out and bogged the waste up until it looked like a comic field dressing, but crucially it stopped the leak. Oh. Simple as that then was disaster averted, but it left me wobbly legged and looking like I'd been in a car crash all the same.

A little while after this trauma, whilst enjoying a 'test' bath, I became aware that he had actually put the taps on the wrong way round. So the hot water came out of the cold tap and vice versa.

You can imagine I didn't have the heart to tell him.

Simultaneously to all this, I had the landscapers in.

A bunch of loveable rogues you would never want to meet (just kidding, they were great lads and I got to learn some new swear words from them too, which was nice).

Their job was to make a combined seating, eating, bbq and fire pit enclosed garden. Fence and contain the goats and tidy up the driveways. God they worked hard, yet they only managed to succeed with 2 out of 3 of these jobs.

The goats whole heartedly took up a kind of Crystal Maze challenge with the landscapers' efforts, using a two pronged strategy of Billy jumping over everything and Jimmy squeezing under everything. They'd even started breaking into the house at this point by jumping up at the door handle and pushing it down. The little bastards.

Inevitably, it's fair to say the goats had us all beaten. We gave up after weeks of attempted containment and ended up shoving them in the newly reinforced chicken coop. It took them a whole week to eat the roof off their new house, which I still have not repaired. It's the only pathetic scrap of payback I could think of for them, as I did indeed spend about £5k on fencing that proved ineffective against little baby Pygmy goats.

I was getting close to being Airbnb ready. All new Egyptian cotton bedding, duck feather duvets and pillows, 40 Egyptian cotton towels all purchased and good to go. The kitchen match fit with tons of new crockery and cutlery (I couldn't use my existing crockery as I had made it all myself. A few years previously I realised I was running out of plates. So I bought a kiln and made my own. Back to taking the hard way round things I hear you mutter)

My stress levels were competing with my excitement levels at this stage, both being off the chart. It was just at this point that the celebrity chefs (or rather their production team) cancelled the booking with me.

They had cancelled and I felt like I'd been jilted at the alter. I know I shouldn't take things to heart so much, it is a downfall of mine. I just put so much effort in and feel so positive about things that when I get let down or disappointed, I fall really hard. It felt at that stage all my efforts at turning my home into a viable earning business was complete folly.

I made my mantra 'be brave, just keep going' boot in to full effect.

The first guests didn't cancel, they actually checked in and I was suddenly rendered homeless. It felt as if I immediately became suspended in animation. All that work, chaos, grief and expense. Now nothing! All that work completed and I now found myself sitting on a mattress in my studio. My boat was still on a trailer and would be for some time yet as there was a load left to do. I was exhausted. I needed some time out and I missed boat life terribly.

CHAPTER 10

BOAT INTERIORS AND BLOW JOBS

Baby's Got Sauce – G. Love and Special Sauce

Thorn in My Pride – Black Crowes

Powder Blue – Elbow

It was Easter, the start of the new boating season, when winter repairs and stoppages get lifted and boats begin moving freely around the network again.

I was desperate to be back on the water. Luckily some friends were out and allowed me to jump on their boat with them. That's 5 people on a 4 berth boat, so that's me sleeping on the kitchen floor. I'll take that, it was a small price to pay.

Their plans were to complete a canal circuit called The Cheshire Ring. 27 locks had to be negotiated in one day as the neighbourhoods we were cruising through were notoriously antisocial, the canal barely navigable due to impossibly random detritus* being thrown in. A giant watery skip for the locals it seemed. But also made tricky by the erm characters that you came across. Mostly wrecked men partying on or sleeping on the lock gates.

We set off from Castlefield basin**, Manchester at 6am Easter Saturday. It's a fascinating section of canal that navigates in between and actually under the towering buildings of downtown Manchester, under roads, through tunnels and underground locks, barely noticed by the commuters and shoppers on the streets above.

*Some particularly notable items untangled and dragged from around friends' props have been a jacket, trousers and underwear, then the suitcase they must have come out of. Tents. Sofas. Mattresses. I once saw a large dolls head severed from its plastic body that gave me such a fright thinking it was a maimed baby I still get palpitations to this day.

**Castlefield Basin, a beautiful place to moor and free of charge accommodation in the heart of the city, but also a fabulous venue site. Part of the canal basin gets boarded over for bands to gig on, it's an amazing transformation and part of the random repurposing of the network I love so much.

This section also includes Canal Street, pretty obviously. Part of the Gay Village of Manchester. The underground locks here are renowned as being secluded hangouts for 'immoral' and 'lewd' behaviour. Indeed there are signs up warning of prosecution to this effect.

As we are waiting for a lock to fill up we're aware of 2 men on the towpath. Next thing they start snogging, no problem with that.

As we open the lock and navigate closer, it becomes apparent one of the men now has his pants down and the other one is on his knees going full steam.

Oh my god! Was it the act or the 7am thing that shocked me? It was absolutely bloody hilarious.

Feeling rejuvenated and completely cheered up (a blow job can do that, sorry am just making myself laugh writing that) the Airbnb up and running, I could finally get back to finishing the boat and getting her launched.

I was pretty anxious about the launch. There was no way of testing the engine as it couldn't be run without being in the water due to the cooling process of the engine. There was no way of knowing if the stern gland / prop shaft (get me sounding all boaty! What I actually mean is the bit that sticks out at the back of the engine bay and into the water) would leak and it was impossible to tell if the ballast was correct. Given the fact that I had a monumentally heavy fit port side it would be a miracle if she didn't just roll over onto her side as she hit the water.

I was also bricking it about my ability to actually sail her. On this boat there are 2 sticks on the side of the control panel and I had no idea what they were supposed to do. I was also in complete denial about actually stopping the boat and mooring up, which I had done little to none of in the past.

I was relying on my boat mate who had helped and supported me on the journey so far. He was going to be with me at launch he promised. Great, I felt reassured on that count at least.

It was now time for me to start on the interior decoration of the boat, I'd been dying to get my teeth into this part of the refit.

The colours I had been inspired to use came from a source not entirely obvious. My good friend Jules on whose boat I had spent Easter, posted a sunrise photo on the BWC* group chat.

*BWC, or 'Bad Wive's Club' as our regular Friday early doors at the pub was named. Named by a particularly disgruntled husband at the time. Alas he is now a former husband, as are the rest of them. So the attempt at a derogatory title for us was singularly insightful as it turned out. We still catch up on occasional Fridays, boat life depending, with most of us humphing down at a table in the pub with an opening line of 'Fuck me, what a day.' or 'You'll never guess what happened.'

Jel's missing from this now, so it is of course a little more subdued, rather than the robust banter it once was.

It was the colours of that sunrise that got me. I love colour passionately. It has the power to alter moods, create environments, inspire. And it's everywhere. Cut into a fig. The harmonies of greens and purples that are within it are truly beautiful.

The decoration for the kitchen and living areas were to have layers of tonally similar colours, pink, pale blue and lilac, all inspired by that sunrise. And white.

I often compare using colour to that of cooking. You can create mood with colours just as you can create flavour with different tastes. I often use white in my interior decoration, that way you can see the different colours more clearly, the white cuts through them, rather like salt does in a casserole. You might think this a bit whimsical, but it's what I go with when consulting with a client and the analogy seems to work well.

The 'flow through' of colour had to work too. As you moved through the boat, or looked through the boat in my case, as it was only 17' long inside, it had to be pleasing to the eye. No jarring change of direction. The bedroom was to be a clean and airy pale turquoise. The tricky one was the bathroom. I ended up going for a pale green then applying a pearlescent paint effect over the top to create a more sympathetic finish to the bathroom walls to go with the flamingo panels. I also love using pink and green together, a great colour combination.

All these colours were in my head, not on a colour card that I could chose from. Therefore I had to hand mix each bespoke colour. I made sure they were tonally correct* and mixed them into the appropriate paint bases. All by hand (yes, before you ask, 50% of the time I run out of paint before I finish, a true professional, me)

*Here's a tip for you if you want to make sure the colours you have chosen are the same in tone, enabling a pleasing flow through of layered colour within a room. Squint. Squint at the colours collected together. This takes the distracting actual colour away, bleaching it out and leaves the depth of tone instead. If they all look pretty similar when you've squinted at them, they're all tonally similar.

CHAPTER 11

Early Life

It was 1983. I was back living at home with my Mum and 3 feral younger siblings. My Mum was an antique dealer and in 1983 it was all about stripped pine. Stripped pine doors, dressers, bedding boxes, everything got stripped. To do this required a huge metal bath filled with diluted caustic acid, warmed up to create fumes adding to the toxic environment. The furniture was lowered into the tank, left to bubble then hauled out and pressure washed off. The pressure washing was always tricky as all the acid softened lead paint would splatter up your body and into your face. The health and safety aspect that was used to counteract this noxious line of work took the form of rubber gloves, apron and wellies…and that's it, a long way off today's standards.

Then there was the refinishing. Sanding and waxing. The wax was particularly entertaining as it contained toluene, a highly flammable and intoxicating substance (they've banned it now, sadly.)

Guess who took the job on ?

Yep. I actually made it into a business. My first business aged 18. Shittest job I could possibly dream up for myself.

I grafted away at this shit job until I had saved up enough money to put a deposit down on my first house, which became mine just before my 19th birthday.

I paid £19K for this mid terraced house, where my interior design passion kicked in to full effect.

I also think it was about then that a salesman knocked on the door and asked me if my Mum was in. No one of my age had their own house then and he assumed it was my parent's home.

It was at this point I started experimenting with paint effects. Putting paint onto furniture instead of stripping it off.

At college my particular interest had been colour and surface pattern. Which I applied whole heartedly to painting furniture. I remember being chuffed to bits with my 1930's bedroom furniture set, all painted up to look like pale grey granite.

For my 21st birthday, my aunt gave me £210. A fortune in 1987 and I spent it all on a spectacular Sanderson giant peony wallpaper with a black background that I papered the hall, stairs and landing with.

This was the start of pushing the boundaries of paint, colour and design for me. I wasn't at Art College anymore, but I was still learning, following an unseen path it seemed. I also had Jelly to bounce off. We bounced all our creative ideas off each other. She was at art college, training to be a ceramicist. I'm surprised they let her stay after setting the college skip fully on fire, melting the metal, having half a dozen fire fighting appliances come and sort her mess out.

We used to help each other out with our fledgling businesses in a practical way too. Once Jel had a stand at the Royal Lancashire Show selling her ceramic pigs (she had a Vietnamese Pot-bellied Pig called Jezebel who was her muse and model, typical of Jel to have a pig as muse.) anyway, I was looking after her stand whilst she went sketching the animals in the pens. A radio presenter approached me believing I was Jelly and asked if he could do an interview. Sure, I said, then proceeded to bullshit my way through Jel's creative and practical process concerning Raku. (Raku? What the fuck was Raku?) The whole interview was aired over the public address system to the multi thousands of people attending the show. She never quite lived that one down, or let me forget it.

A year or so later, after I had finished the house, I was beginning to get jaded with pine stripping as the market was sliding and I was starting to lose money. Cash flow was a constant struggle and the minefields of accounts, taxes and bills was really beginning to eat at me.

My Mum and brother had diversified into antique export and had opened a shop in Los Angeles and I wanted to expand my horizons too (okay, pay my debts off before they became unmanageable was closer to reality)

It was time to sell the house. I wasn't expecting to have to do this so soon, I wanted to enjoy the fruits of my labour for at least a while, but I had no option. I didn't want debt to break me.

I still don't like debt even now, which is bloody ironic given the boat money pit I now have.

I put the house on the market, I remember one of my Mum's friends saying if I got the asking price of £38K, 3 years after I had bought it, he would run down Wigan high street naked.

I sold the house for £38K. He was too pissed off with envy to carry out his threat. Dickhead. Some men just could not fathom how a 21-year-old girl could manage all this on her own. Truth is, neither could I.

Before I knew it, I was homeless again. I'd paid my debts off, rammed my car with all my possessions and tried to figure out what I was going to do next.

With or Without You – U2

Behind the Mask – Eric Clapton

Addicted to Love – Robert Palmer

CHAPTER 12

LAUNCH AND TRAUMA

Walk the Walk – Gaz Coombes

Destiny – Zero 7

Trouble – Ray La Montagne

The boat interior was beginning to look exactly as I had it in my mind's eye. 70's style lockers and cupboards set off by a beautiful baby blue retro fridge which cost the same as a small car (not married anymore so don't give a fuck about the cost of something so beautiful. Actually come to think of it, I didn't give a fuck about it whilst I was married either, maybe another part of my downfall, that one)

I used blinds on the windows but because the gas cooker was positioned underneath part of the kitchen window, it meant that the blind had to be up to use the hob due to fire hazard, so I had to obscure the glass in the window with a kind of sticky backed plastic, for privacy.

If I wanted to make a cup of tea naked in the morning (don't picture it, it could give you indigestion) I wouldn't be scarring any random dog walkers. It also ensured I couldn't see the dogs of the random walkers crapping on my mooring lines, which always started a morning badly.

Of course I managed to find the most beautiful and the most expensive artist created window film in the Western Hemisphere, where it's purchased by the square centimetre, yes, really.

The window was out anyway due to leakage problems (again) so I was able to bench it to make absolutely sure I adhered the plutonium priced window film correctly to the oddly shaped kitchen window.

Of course it was going to go wrong, how was that ever going to go well? I templated and cut the film the opposite way round. It wouldn't fit on the curved shaped glazed ends of the window. Jesus, I couldn't make it go worse if I had been blindfolded and given a bread knife to cut it with. I didn't have time to order and wait for more film to be delivered as the window had to go back in. So I dodged it and patched it. Amazingly, it looked fine, the design on the film hid my hack job. TFFT.

It was time for the boat to have a final seal test. She was going in the water no matter what but I wanted to know the extent of my problems (Pah! That's a laugh knowing what I know now).

My boat mate had given me a date that was convenient for him to help me launch. Tension and stress was running high within me but manageable as I knew I had his support.

The boat failed the seal test again, but not as profoundly. Whatever, I was over it. I had bigger fish to fry. I had no bathroom. The flamingo panels weren't ready which wasn't a deal breaker. However having no working toilet definitely was and no one could work out why which just added to the frustration.

Launch date was looming. Stress was building. Added to this, at the last minute the boat insurance company, although banking my payment a month previously mentioned in passing that the boat wouldn't be insured without a full survey because of her age. Great. How much was that going to cost and how quickly could I find and employ a surveyor?

It was Friday May 13th appropriately when the surveyor came out, launch day was Tuesday 17th. The brand new toilet still wasn't working for some unfathomable reason but that paled into insignificance when I got my next bombshell.

I hadn't heard from boat mate. I knew he was on his boat. I had already arranged with him that I'd do the 3 hour round trip to pick him up, launch the boat then deliver him back. Still, he'd gone quiet and it was starting to make me nervous.

There's no way he'd let me down as he knew how much it meant to me. There must be another reason. I text him to see if he was okay and confirm we were good to go.

He was fine, but 'it wasn't convenient' to help me launch the boat. Wasn't convenient??

The arse fell out of my world. As you know I suffer terribly if I'm let down or disappointed. Jesus the tears I cried. How could he do that? There must be an extenuating circumstance that he's not telling me about.

Nope, there wasn't. It was simply not convenient for him. Arsehole.

I know you'll be saying at this stage why get so upset? I have no idea why I do it but I end up braving it so much in life. Pushing myself with challenges - climbing mountains on my own, volunteering in orphanages, buying a bloody narrowboat.

My theory is that no one will do it for you. It goes back to that Mark Twain quote '20 years from now you will regret the things that you didn't do rather than the things you did' Bloody haunts me that phrase as it's exactly true.

Right. Pick myself up. Find another way, another someone to help. Of course everyone that had any knowledge of raw water engines and the eccentricities of old boats were busy at such short notice.

Eventually I got a nice new boater friend to agree to help me. So I felt a little better not least because I had my lovely son Ted for moral support, who's always there for me. Gorgeous boy.

Launch day on the Lancaster Canal at Garstang arrived. At long last. I was bricking it, the myriad of potential problems were bubbling very near the surface making me dangerously close to crying which I desperately did not want to do. How ridiculous and over dramatic would that look? Jelly kept phoning me, she knew how panicked I was, knew how much this had cost me mentally and physically as she had supported me every single step of the way, even when I was wrong.

The boat was strapped down to the trailer, hooked up to a tractor and off she went to the marina, me following nervously in my car, 26 weeks after I bought her and nearly 300% over budget. Here's me thinking it would take 10 weeks to flip a narrowboat. How hard could it be really? (Dickhead)

As we pulled into the marina, just at my most tense, I saw a familiar face. Jelly. She had set off at 6am to get there before me and had been hiding in the café for hours, waiting. She wasn't ever going to let me go through this alone, she said. My best friend in all the world.

A War Of The Worlds looking mad sling piece of machinery was used to gingerly lift her off the trailer and into the water at the marina. I'd asked the crane driver to leave her in the sling in the water as I had no idea what was going to happen.

Once in the water she immediately and quite dramatically listed port side. That bloody 18mm ply fit was indeed over balancing the boat. Mercifully the skin fittings I'd drilled in the hull for domestic drainage were clear of the water (well, only just on port side)

Okay, lets get her started up. Boat helper was struggling. Out came the manuals. Still nothing. The engine would not start and the battery was flattening faster than a popped balloon. At this point the thought of crying had completely left me to be replaced with a low screaming inside my brain.

After a torturous hour watching a well intentioned man struggle and crumble before me (probably something to do with Jelly giving him a death stare) I decided to take control and find an engineer to help, this was a marina after all right?

I have a lot of faith in thinking that mostly in life for every negative you encounter a positive will present itself. My positive came in the form of Big John. The Engineer. Think of a cross between Lee Van Cleef and John Wayne and you're nearly there. But from Burnley. He had just pulled onto the yard as I was walking over to find someone. He simply jumped aboard fiddled about a bit and fired her up. Voila! An absolute bloody miracle. Little did I know that John's expertise and all the rest of my money would be required for the whole spectrum of mechanical and user error problems that would occur in the months that lay ahead.

I would never have found John if I hadn't been let down in the first place, I do love that about life.

For now though, I was finally on the water and my god, that engine sounded beautiful.

CHAPTER 13

USER ERROR

Trust the Sun – Elbow

The Strange Museum – Paul Weller

Release the Pressure – Leftfield

After the drama of actually getting her launched, then nearly crashing into a yoghurt pot* as I came out of the marina (turns out I was using the gear and accelerator levers in the exact opposite way than I should have been. No surprise really as I don't even know my left from right. I have to wiggle my hand around to check which is which) I started to get the hang of it. Well, the going forwards bit. Not the stopping or pulling the boat in bit. I did however do a very fine donut to turn her around (full disclosure, big turning point on the canal, little boat and I hadn't mastered the art of reversing and doing a 3 point turn)

The prop shaft had begun to leak and she was profoundly listing to the (wiggle hand) left, but I was determined not to let these minor problems get me down.

*Yoghurt pot is the ever so slightly piss taking and derogatory name for fiberglass cruisers. It's a mutual thing really. The cruisers look down their noses at us pikey boaters and us pikey boaters just think cruisers are rubbish boats with no respect for any speed limits. This is a generalisation and not meant be taken too seriously, before anyone gets their knickers in a twist, by the way.

Ted and I moored up (having assumed the brace position first) and I got to practice whacking mooring pins in and tying knots. All good. My first night on the boat. I also got to try out the split door design I mentioned earlier. The one where the sofa bed is pulled out and the top part of the back door opens inwards over it. Enabling me sitting out drinking cider on the back deck to get over the bed and go for a wee. I encountered my first design flaw at this point. You can't open the door if your son is asleep on the sofa bed. Well, you can, but you get to hear a lot of swear words whilst you attempt it.

Over the next couple of days my mission was to sort the ballast out (I was in a kind of panicked denial about the leaky prop shaft at that point). I put over 70 kilos of anything heavy I could find into the right hand side of the boat. Lead flashing, dumbbells and a dirty great big heavy curb stone, which was ridiculously heavy and something I definitely needed help lifting. I grabbed what I thought was a nice unassuming man working on a boat nearby on the towpath and got him to half kill himself by carrying and lifting it into my engine bay.

Turns out that man became my new boat mate. On reflection I should have called him Jonah, however I named him Monkey as he was cack handedly entertaining from the off.

I ended up putting a massive 150kgs ballast in, with that and the heavy refit I'm amazed I didn't nearly sink her that first week.

I left that until the second week…

Anyway, I whole heartedly threw myself in to learning how to move the boat. Everyone else seemed to manage it fine. How hard could it be?

It was trickier than I thought actually. I hadn't realised crash mooring was a skill that could be embraced so easily and I was bloody great at it.

I kept practicing though. I was informed by many that my little boat could be turned around on the canal "anywhere". The lying bastards. I proved them all wrong by trying it.

One turning attempt that comes to mind was when I ended up off roading, if you can do such a thing on a boat, by mounting a sand bank, panicking, whacking the revs right up and bouncing back off the bank and back on my way again,

This was the beginning of many nervy poos I was going to need in the next few months, I can tell you.

Because of this epic fail in turning 'anywhere' I ended up having to go right up to the next winding hole* to turn her round. Then as I reached my chosen mooring spot after another hour of cruising, I panicked again trying to moor her up, did everything wrong and ended up going to yet another bloody winding hole to do the exact same thing again, adding 2 whole hours to my trip out.

I added shredded nerves as well as nervy poos to my ever increasing skill set and it was still only week 1.

*Winding hole is a wider expanse of the canal that allows boats to do a 3 point turn.

Another good one 11 days in, was missing the winding hole (I thought it was someone's back garden water feature, honestly) so I had a go again at turning the boat on a wide bit of the canal. Turns out it was a shallow bit too. I ran the boat completely aground. Couldn't pole her off the bank, I was stuck fast.

Absolutely sod it, I turned the engine off. If I'd had a cigar I would have smoked it, a complete Hamlet moment. Anyway, turn it around and look at the positives Emma. I needed to stop the boat anyway as I wanted a wee, the sun was shining, I could pour a cider, make some lunch and wait for a boat to come past and tow me off.

A boat did come passed eventually. A big cruiser. I flagged him down (kind of, he must have been doing at least 60 miles an hour).

'Can you please tow me off this bank? I'm on my own and I'm stuck'

'No chance' he said, 'get someone else to do it'. And off he sped. Fucking yoghurt pot bastard.

I eventually poled the boat off the bank using the wake he left that was still going 10 minutes later and turned the boat at the same time.

I recovered from that drama and realised it was starting to get late. I wasn't sure where I could moor as large stretches were weedy and unmoorable. I was beginning to get anxious and really tired. I had sailed a lot further than I had done before. There were also other problems with the boat. The prop shaft was leaking worse than ever although Big John had repacked it. I'd managed to drain all my new batteries. The solar panel didn't seem to be working so I had no power at all, also no water as I needed electric to power the water pump. I'd also managed to pull all the knobs off my brand new cooker (how the hell had I even managed that?)

Panic was setting in just as I came across her. NB (Narrowboat) Liberty. I'd met her owners at the marina as I launched a mere few days previously.

They came to my rescue. Robert pulled me in with the line I'd thrown him and moored me up. I had a tearful meltdown of thanks to him whilst he politely backed away making me promise to come over and eat with him and his wife. Which I gratefully did and man alive it was one of the best towpath barbecues I'd ever had.

And there you have it. The kindness of strangers on the cut. There will always be problems and there will always be people to help you. It's a level playing field which I absolutely adore. I even include the cruisers in this! (well, apart from the fat bastard earlier on that day of course).

It's just as well I'd been looked after, fed and was rested. Because the day after, it got a lot worse.

I got up the morning after, feeling slightly psychologically bruised and went to check the leak status in the engine bay. Oh my god. There was now a steady flow of canal water coming into the boat. I bailed as much water as I could out, but I knew this was bad, very bad.

CHAPTER 13

BAD BREAKDOWNS

Soul Suckers – Amos Lee

Shut Your Eyes – Snow Patrol

My Very Best' – Elbow

I limped the boat back. It was a Sunday and I didn't want to disturb John about it. I decided to get to the closest mooring to a road so that he could get to me more easily with all his tools. But it was too late for that. My beautiful Dawn Piper was going to sink. 13 days after launch.

I phoned the Marina where I had originally launched from and begged for an emergency lift out the next morning (there's a long waiting list to use the crane sling but I managed to beg a slot with them)

I called Monkey. I needed his help. I had to get her pumped out. But I had no power to fire up my wet vac to pump the engine bay out. I had to borrow his generator, his diesel and his battery charger. In order to do that I had to pull him out of the pub half pissed, take him to the marina and the boat he was working on, load up, get it all to my boat and set up. Then return him back to the pub. Jesus. Robbie Cummings* never had this shit to deal with did he?

*Robbie Cummings is the 'god of all canal things' and presenter of a TV canal series.

It's fair to say I had an uneasy nights sleep. I couldn't use the genny past 8pm as it would disturb my boat neighbours. So I had to keep scooping the water out with a bucket.

I had reneged and contacted John who was extremely reassuring and was set to mend her as soon as I was in dry dock again. This was not going to be cheap though.

I had also been told that I would have to reverse my boat into the marina in order to face the right way for craning out. Well that wasn't going to happen. With my boat skills I could barely go forwards. I sailed in forwards the next morning. In the torrential rain which emulated my crying heart and still crashed into the jetty a bit. I must also have been on nervy poo x 4 by then.

So out she came. Back on dry land again. This boat was becoming more like an expensive wheel-less caravan by the day. At least I couldn't crash her or sink her at this point.

I have to admit though, I walked away that day. I didn't even lock her up. I'd absolutely had enough. I couldn't take any more boat trauma. Or nervy poos for that matter.

It was now up to John and his fantastically capable and mental wife Julie to fix her.

Oh my god. Just how much damage can you do to a boat in 13 days? Really?

It turned out that all the stern gear was knackered. (I didn't know what all that was either)

So that's a new prop shaft. New bushes and god, all sorts of other expensive engineery stuff.

I had totally buggered my brand new batteries so they had to be replaced and twice as many added because I was likely to do it again I was told. (They must think I'm an idiot…) Including all the connections and trays. The whole wiring loom needed to be replaced because the main fuses from the batteries had been swapped for a metal bar which was a quicker and more effective way of starting a fire on the boat rather than throwing petrol and a match on it. New control panel, bilge pump, alternator.

I actually phased out of all the things that needed fixing beyond this point.

John was having hell on trying to get the old stern gear out. Days and days worth of labour just to remove the broken stuff. And my cooker knobs still remained firmly broken.

But who cares? Because the flamingos were at long last ready! My shower panels could now be fitted. The cherry on the collapsed cake. They were an absolute bugger to fit of course.

When Gary and I had finished struggling, wrestling and swearing with them it was time for the final reveal. Taking the obscured protective film off. Man alive they were truly fantastic, exactly as I had hoped they would be. Totally couldn't believe I'd actually pulled it off from the beginnings of an idea in my tiny mind.

So that's the shower working then. Ah, hang on. It appears there's a massive leak on the shower plumbing.

Oh for fucks sake.

I felt like putting that metal bar back in, setting fire to her and going and reloading Tinder.

I left the team to it. I couldn't cope with any more. Besides, the Airbnb was going well and needed my attention. I also had a big Verre Eglomise commission to complete. Just as well as this was going to cost literally thousands of pounds.

Full disclosure, I did reload Tinder.

I managed to find a proper fitty.

(Tinder tip : never go for the really good looking ones or the really fit ones, they're without exception high maintenance and hard work) Why do I never take my own advice?

Ooh. That reminds me of a Tinder story for you. A year earlier I agreed to meet a good looking guy for lunch at a local pub. Now, don't judge me on this, it's just a habit I've got that I don't seem able to break. I'm used to working on site. I'm also used to other (always male) trades bending over fixing things right next to me. I always check out their arses. Specifically what pants they're wearing (I'm not proud of myself) But I've got it to such a fine art I can tell you what trade they are by the quality of their underwear (FYI electricians wear the Calvin Kleins)

On this date it was my turn to go the bar and whilst I was walking back to the table, I checked out his pants.

He was wearing ladies pink silky knickers. I kid you not. Bloody Tinder.

CHAPTER 14

Early Life

I had sold the house, paid my debts off and began looking for another one to buy. Finances were tricky. I was self employed with a business that I was changing direction with. If I was going to get a mortgage it would have to be on 'self certification' and it was going to take time, meanwhile I had nowhere to live.

My friend's dairy farmer Mum stepped in (I'd run away from home when I was 12 and supposedly unbeknown to her, slept in her barn for 3 nights, so she knew the format well).

Just before Christmas 1988 at 22 years old, I moved into the upstairs store room of the dairy wash house. One room, no kitchen, no bathroom. Just an outside loo that the farmhands used. I was of course, very grateful. However, it was a stark change from the house I had just spent every available moment doing up and every available pound note on, to make the loveliest of homes for myself and maybe, just maybe, a potential family.

I had originally felt I was beginning to climb the ladder towards that promise I made to myself just 7 years previously from my cell in the convent.

Instead of this though, I dusted off the the suitcase containing all my treasures, decorated the sparse room and erected a giant Christmas tree which took up a third of the floor space. Never one to be constrained by a limited interior and always going for maximum effect, clearly.

The Christmas tree fell over and crashed onto me in the middle of the night and I realised I may have pushed things a little too far.

I really had to find a do-upper house to buy and soon, I was struggling living this way. Which was a lot easier said than done.

Faith – George Michael

Cry – Godley and Crème

Diamond Life – Sade

CHAPTER 15

RELAUNCH

Sweet Disposition – Temper Trap

You Give Me Something – James Morrison

Little by little – Groove Armada

It took 3 weeks for John and Julie to repair her. An amazing achievement as the prop shaft, bushes and other bits needed to be bespoke made. Gary had repaired the leak, completed the bathroom and had even glued my cooker knobs back on, bless him. I was good for relaunch.

So on 18th June 2022 my lovely Dawn Piper was put back in the water. John had done an absolutely superb job on her.

I fired her up, she sounded perfect and off I went. Back along the Lanky (The Lancaster Canal) fully repaired and rejuvenated.

It lasted 20 minutes. She broke down. A hose had split and was jetting hot water into the engine bay. Noooo!!

Of course it would have been easy if I'd had tools on board, which of course I didn't.

I was going to have to go back to basics. Again. I reasoned that every time I'd needed to change a plug (it was a thing 25 years ago) I never had a screwdriver to hand, but I always had a butter knife available. A butter knife it was then. I unscrewed the jubilee clip with it, cut off the damaged hose with my kitchen scissors, expanded the hose to be refitted with a mug of hot water and retightened the clip with my butter knife. Hooray! I am a boat fixing genius!

The next week was bliss. Sunny, dreamy and perfect boating. My daughter Kitty and her boyfriend Jake jumped on. We sailed to the pub (mandatory requirement of any boating trip) We barbecued on the towpath (same). Got drunk, danced. This was what all the hard work, tears and expense was for.

Also , the aim of having my children and extended family on board and enjoying it as much as I, was incredibly richly rewarding and everything I had hoped to achieve.

I started to relax at last. The joy I had yearned for was now beginning to envelope me.

One particularly lovely day whilst at one of my favourite moorings on the Lanky called the Lambing Fields (I love all the different names that boaters have given to moorings that get passed along the towpath and along the years becoming part of the integral network of the canal system), I was sitting on the back deck eating lunch, listening to music watching the moorhens busying themselves and feeding their babies. When I sensed rather than saw someone walk past the boat. I turned round to watch a man with long white hair strolling along the towpath, totally naked! You have never seen a person move as fast as me by grabbing my phone and taking a photo. I just couldn't not take the shot. No one would believe I had just seen Father Christmas on his summer holidays walking naked down the towpath!! God I love the cut for the absolutely random slices of life you see.

Another day saw me pottering along on the boat when I passed a pair of swans. They must have had a domestic between them as they were in a terrible temper, trying to face off with the boat, hissing, flapping their giant wings. I'd just got beyond them when I saw a couple of blokes in a kayak coming my way. I slowed down so my wake wouldn't upset them then took a little time out to watch the swans trying to sink them (I did warn them but they were very blokey and offhand about it) It was totally hilarious watching them trying to out-paddle a pair of angry swans who were virtually on the back of the kayak hissing at them. God I love the cut.

CHAPTER 16

THE KINDNESS OF STRANGERS

F.E.A.R. – Ian Brown

Moving – Super Grass

Trading Air - Athlete

Just as I had relaxed and was getting a little more confident with moving (and stopping) the boat, there was more trouble.

Monkey and I were out on another afternoon jaunt on the cut. I was always checking the temperature gauge as I was completely paranoid about the engine over-heating. Just as well as on this particular day the gauge had risen quickly and alarmingly high. I checked to see if the pump was spitting the heated water out back into the canal, it wasn't. That's a bad sign. That means that water wasn't being pumped into the engine to cool it down. A very bad sign indeed.

In fact so bad I had to cut the engine immediately before I'd even had chance to pull her in to the side. I couldn't allow the engine to get any hotter as I would have blown the head gasket*

*I know this one well as every car I have ever owned up to about 12 years ago, I have blown the head gasket.

When I was in Sri Lanka a couple of years previously, the taxi driver was being a complete arse with me trying to charge me more for using his air conditioning in the melting hot vehicle which naturally I refused to do. Next thing, he's had to pull over. His car had over-heated. It was me, the stupid white western female that diagnosed the head gasket problem, carefully took the radiator cap off and filled it with my own drinking water. Then I explained to him that the radiator cap had to be left off to prevent pressure building and to drive slowly to the next village which was miles away to get it fixed. Nobhead. He was a lot nicer to me after that though.

So there we were. Slowly drifting into the bushes. Just bloody great. This was the first of many, and I mean many, times I had to get the barge pole off the roof and pole the boat out of the off-side bushes and onto the near-side tow path.

In fact I used that pole so often to move my over-heated boat that summer on the Lanky, she was resembling a gondola. Much to the entertainment of passers by, until I got them to catch my centre line rope and pull me in that is. To be honest everyone I met was absolutely great with me.

One particular time that stands out was when I had moored in a beautiful rural spot for the night and was returning the boat to Monkey's private moorings that he had lent me for my Lanky stay* as his boat was in dry dock.

*The Lanky is an autonomous canal. In order to get on or off this canal, you had to cross the dreaded Ribble Link. An intimidating 7 mile section of tidal river encompassing sea, river and canal locks. A crossing I was going to have to make at some point in the summer in order to join the main canal network. I was still in absolute denial about this. All the breakdowns along with the single cylinder historic engine and my helmsman skills, I felt denial was a fair place to be.

I was cruising through a lovely section of canal where both banks were fully overgrown with white Meadowsweet, Yellow Iris and Purple Loosestrife when the engine just cut out. Dead. She had been running hot again but it was manageable. She had never just died though. Once again, I found myself lodged in the bushes. Except this time it was early on a Sunday morning and even if there was a passer by, they couldn't get to my rope. I couldn't pole myself to the side either as the towpath was inaccessible because of the beautiful wild flowers which suddenly were not looking that beautiful any more. I doubted very much there would be a boat along as it was so early and rural. I decided to use my begging skills once again (these were much more refined than my boating skills). I put a shout out on the Lancaster Canal Users Facebook. I had broken down. Could anyone possibly come out and tow me to my mooring?

A general rule of thumb would be, if you're going to breakdown try and do it on the Lanky as the boaters on there are so lovely (have to be as they all keep passing each other going up and down the canal; nowhere to run!)

NB Huffler came to my rescue. A beautiful 60' (exactly twice my size) boat with a fabulous 90 year old twin cylinder Gardner engine owned by husband and wife octogenarians, Tony and Margaret.

As Huffler was making her way to me a giant widebeam* came hurtling towards me heading downstream. I flagged him down and asked for a tow to the winding hole. At least that would make it easier for Tony by not having to reverse up to me.

*Widebeam boats are massive. Between 10' and 12' wide (derogatory term used for these boats is 'Fat Arse') This particular one was owned by a notoriously flashy and arrogant man that thought he was actually on a speed boat.

I threw him my bow line that he attached to his stern, leaving a long length in between us. Then he set off at breakneck speed. Fuck me it was like I was water skiing. My little boat was careening from side to side, bouncing off bushes, over mud banks in a totally chaotic and scary way. He released me at the winding hole where I broadsided to a halt under a nearby bridge. Jesus, remind me never to do that again.

At least I could now moor up, compose myself and wait for Tony and Margaret on Huffler to arrive.

Which they duly did and what a totally different experience it was to the one I'd just had. Calm, organised and incredibly professional, as if these 80 year olds rescued stranded boats every day. Tony showed me how to tie the boat 'off' instead of 'on' so that it would be easier to untie. He also showed me how to tie a spring line so that the boats didn't scissor next each other as Huffler had breasted up to me (tied me to her side) All the while Margaret shimmied along the gunwales of the boat like a teenager tying my bow line to Huffler's centre line.

We were now nearly 14' wide as Tony carefully navigated both boats along, Margaret at the bow keeping lookout for any boats coming towards us as we now pretty much filled the width of the canal. It was exciting stuff, a really interesting and enjoyable experience, especially compared to the one I could have had if I'd continued with that widebeam.

Also a cunning plan was forming in my tiny mind. Huffler was booked to come across the Ribble Link at the beginning of August. I'd be warned that I would need a tow across or at least be tied to another boat. Left to cross unaided would be like throwing a chipolata into a jacuzzi and hoping for the best. With my luck and skill set I'd end up with the boat upside down and on her way to Ireland.

I decided to plead my case. Tony and Margaret didn't bat an eyelid. Of course they would tow me. No trouble to them, they'd crossed the Link plenty of times. I booked the crossing and my relief was palpable.

CHAPTER 17

GOOD BREAKDOWNS

One Day Like This – Elbow

The only song to resonate with this chapter in my life.

It was approaching my birthday. My kids were joining me for a sail from my moorings to a nearby town, Garstang, where we'd hit a couple of pubs, go to a nice restaurant for lunch, sail back, barbecue and have a bonfire. This was the pinnacle of a dream come true and achievement for me and I'll tell you for why.

As I'd mentioned at the beginning, I had waited for my kids to be old enough so that I could get divorced. I then had to stabilise us all in order to set in motion a giant hope and dream of mine.

To try and find my first born son, Adam who would be 35 years old at this point. If he was even alive, as I had no way of knowing. My 2 kids Ted and Kitty had known about Adam since they were old enough to grasp the concept of having a missing older half brother. They were about 6 and 8 years old when I told them about Adam. I kind of integrated him into our domestic conversations by making his birthdate the password to the family's laptop. You know the kind of thing. 'Mum what's the password?' 'You know, it's Adam's birthday' It worked well.

A few years previously my friend whom I had first met at the convent, as she was in for the same reason, had instigated the search for her son so I had some knowledge of the convoluted process. (She was older than me, most of the girls were to be fair, had come from a good Catholic family and was unmarried) She had got the nuns to organise her incarceration and subsequent adoption whereas I had gone through social services.

Unbreakable bonds form within traumas and we had always kept in contact.

Her story is amazing. She went on to marry the father of her first born and then have 3 more children. Obviously the search for her first child started early on. Formal adoption agencies were hired, letters sent but nothing came back. He could not or would not be found. She employed private detectives. Still no news. Finally she took the huge decision to go on a TV programme specialising in reuniting families. The final straw. Do you know what? They only went and found him! Thankfully for the sake of his privacy the programme was never made.

It turns out that although the nuns promised my friend that her baby would have a better life than the one she could give him, it seems they had actually given him to the first married couple they could find. With the emphasis on 'married'. He was brought up so near to where she was living with her husband and children that only a train line separated them. All that stopped all of her children going to the same school unbeknown was the train line.

I can delightedly tell you that the whole family are fully reunited and her heart is entirely complete with little grand children popping out all over the place. A 40 year trauma done with. Amazing.

Her story gave me hope yet also gave me huge trepidation. All the obvious questions coming to the fore. Had he been adopted by lovely people? Had he had a good life? Had he been mentally disabled by the trauma of the birth? I was desperately hoping that he was alive and happy.

I enlisted the help of a private adoption agency (there are council run ones, but I'd heard good reports about the lady running this one) and I was assigned an intermediary. A lovely lady called Debbie who would walk me through the procedure, do all the background checks and hopefully make contact.

Sounds straightforward doesn't it? It wasn't.

First of all she needed to get to know me, hear my background story. Make sure I was emotionally stable enough for both mine and my son's sake. I had to prove who I was with my birth certificate which had been misplaced years ago, so I needed to apply for another. I had got Adam's birth certificate though so that was something. Because the adoption took place so long ago there were no digital records so we had an interminable and torturous wait until someone from social services had the time to search through all the years of paper records to find my case. That took months and months.

Then I got the call from Debbie.

No, she'd not found him but she could confirm he was alive.

Full tears and snot meltdown from me. I actually remember the moment. My legs wouldn't support me so I knelt on the floor with my hands over my face and watched the pool of tears and snot grow ever larger on the floor. He was alive! 37 years of not knowing.

She talked me through the next steps. To protect Adam's privacy and emotional stability only 3 letters could be sent to him, not emails as they could easily be construed as spam, if she did indeed find him.

The first letter for Debbie to write would be vague - did he know of a woman from Wrexham (his birthplace) in 1982 (his birth year)? As she is very keen to know of his wellbeing. Simply that. This was just in case he did not know he was adopted or if another member of the household opened it.

Second letter - a letter was sent to you 3 months ago. You may not have received it. The woman from Wrexham is still very keen to know of your wellbeing. I look forward to hearing your response.

Third letter - This is the last letter I shall write to you as I don't want to infringe on your privacy. Enclosed within this letter is another sealed letter from the woman from Wrexham. I understand this might not be the correct time for you to connect. Please be assured that should you choose to now or in the future I will honour your wishes as a formal intermediary.

That was it. If Debbie found him and he didn't respond to the letters, I couldn't take it any further. At least I knew he was alive, I could hold onto that.

She found him. More snot and tears. I was not allowed to know anything about him, not even if his new parents kept his original birth name.

The first letter went out. He Got In Touch. He got in touch! Yes he did know he was adopted. But that was it. Nothing else. Good start though!

The second letter went out 3 months later. Nothing. No response at all.

Debbie decided to bring the 3rd letter forward and send it a month after the second as we hadn't heard anything. I had to construct my letter that she was to include in a sealed envelope. I remember the wording to this day. I kept it succinct but with enough emotion for him to know how I felt. I didn't want to scare him off with a desperate rambling apology. I began my letter that I might never even know that he would read with 'first of all know that you are loved and have always been loved'

The 3rd letter was sent on a Wednesday. Thursday he got in touch. Now there were snot and tears from Debbie as well as me. In fact I'm crying whilst writing this now!

He had been adored by his parents, beautifully looked after, sent to the best schools, was successful in business and love. They had done a superb job and I would be forever grateful to them.

He had no other siblings. So when his parents tragically died years previously, apart from his partner, aunt and uncle, he thought he had no-one.

He now found he not only had a mother but he had a brother and sister too. As well as grandparents, aunts, uncles and cousins.

Don't get me wrong, it's been a bumpy ride. How could it not be? We often resemble a troop of feral monkeys and Adam has a more considered and organised life.

For me though, I felt complete. All that heartbreak for all those years. I now had my missing boy back. My 3 children united at last.

My birthday arrived. Adam jumped on the boat at the moorings and we sailed the hour into Garstang where we met up with Ted, Kit and Jake. We did indeed drink, eat a fabulous lunch and drink a bit more. We then got back on the boat and sailed back to the moorings for more partying. On the way back I thought it a very good idea to show the kids my donut boat turning skills, so proceeded to do a 360" boat spin. Next thing the crew of a cruiser that I assumed was moored started shouting out to me. Shit. What have I done now? I hadn't done anything. Phew. A larger cruiser had sped past them earlier and lodged their boat on a mud bank. They were stranded. Ted threw them my bowline and I towed them off by reversing.

So not only had I reached the pinnacle of happiness and achievement that day by having all my kids together on the boat, it was my 56th birthday and I was a boat saving hero! Hurrah!! The day ended with playing rounders (badly, I accidentally hit Kitty in the face with the bat. Oops) and a barbecue and bonfire. That was a bloody great day.

CHAPTER 18

WATER, WATER, EVERYWHERE

Love You More – Alexi Murdoch

Let Me Down Easy – Paulo Nutini

I'm Yours – Jason Mraz

The following week was a hazy, lazy beautiful boaty one. I had guests in the house so decided to slowly take the boat up to the top of the Lanky, to Tewitfield. The furthest point on the British canal system. She was still running hot but not alarmingly. I moored in Lancaster for the weekend. Met up with old friends I'd not seen in years. Went shopping in vintage markets, and old bookshops (bought the most fab denim jacket with a picture of Frida Kahlo on the back).

Even my usually disgruntled with me land-lubber boyfriend was happy (the fitty from Tinder I told you about, Jesus he was hard work)

Life was sweet.

I sailed up to Hest Bank. This place was on my boating bucket list. You could moor at Hest Bank, walk 5 minutes and be on the beach. How fantastic is that! And that is exactly what I did. I sunbathed on the beach, collected pebbles, read my new books, sketched, I even got my bike off the roof and went exploring. One big overwhelming feeling of wellbeing.

Whilst out on my bike I came across an older gentleman. I'd got off the bike to go under a bridge so we started walking along and chatting. I told him about my boat and he told me about his life as a professional pushbike racer and what the bikes were like in his day. It was lovely. He said he'd always lived by the canal but had never been on a boat. I told him I had to get through the one and only swing bridge later that week and had no idea how to do it. So we did a deal. He would open the swing bridge for me and I would take him for a spin on my boat. We agreed to meet at 10am that Thursday.

However, Alan didn't get on the boat and I didn't get through the swing bridge. Instead I had to emergency sprint the boat right back to her moorings that Thursday as a disaster of alarming proportions had struck.

I could hear a kind of sloshing noise in the boat. The water pump, part of the plumbing system, had been sporadically kicking in but surely if there was a giant leak the pump wouldn't stop? What the hell was going on?

Then I realised the floor was a bit spongy. Oh god. That might signal bad news.

I gingerly peeled back the Lino and lifted the floor panels to reveal a massive paddling pool. Oh my god. I took out what ballast I could and started bailing her out with a mug, but the water didn't look like canal water, it looked fresh, so I wasn't actually sinking then I presumed. There must be a leak. I mopped all the water out, checked for obvious leaks, couldn't find any so deduced that the leak was the dreaded one. The one behind the tiled hearth. The one with the log burner solidly positioned on top of, who's flue went up through the roof of the boat and was firmly and permanently bolted down on to. I couldn't face it. I put the ballast, floor boards and Lino back in position. I had decided to deal with it when I got back to the moorings the week after.

The next day my Mum and her friend were jumping on for a trip out. I intended going up to Carnforth, turning around and bringing them back. She'd made the egg sandwiches so they were good to go on a grannie's big day out.

Whilst I was waiting for them to arrive, I began filling the boat's water tank up. I decided to brave it and check it was still dry under the floorboards. To my absolute horror it was full of water again. I couldn't understand it. I began bailing out. And bailing out. And bailing out. It actually seemed like the boat was filling up faster than I was bailing. What the hell was going on? This was bad.

Hang on. I remembered I still had the hose on, filling the tank up. No, it hadn't come lose and was hosing water into the boat. It was a lot worse than that. The water tank must have ruptured. Oh my shitting Jesus. So that's a very bad leak behind the fireplace AND a ruptured water tank.

I phoned Big John the Engineer on speed dial.

Now John is a very calm man. On this occasion I took it as a very bad sign that he sounded alarmed. I was told I had to bring the boat back to the moorings immediately. An 8 hour sail. By then I had a couple of grannies and their egg sandwiches on board, I had a grandad standing duty at a swing bridge and a boat that had cost as much as the Titanic, but seemed to be even more doomed. Great. I had to find a way round this.

I turned the boat around. The grannies, loving a bit of drama, settled in with a rug on their knees, sat on deck chairs in the front well of the boat and got their fart smelling butties out. I put a shout out on the local Facebook page for someone to please, please go and tell Alan what had happened and get him to stand down from swing bridge duty.

By the time I reached Lancaster, the grannies had finished their butties (thank god), the crisps, the cake and all the biscuits. Man alive those septuagenarians can eat! I hoofed them out there, before they made a start at filling the cassette toilet up and they Ubered back to their car (apparently life's too short to bother getting on a bus with other people)

I made it back to the moorings with just enough daylight left. Knackered, flat and with a feeling of expensive dread in the pit of my stomach. At least I was there and ready for John the next day.

John and his wife Julie duly turned up. I left them to it (just as John was trying not to rip the front end of the boat off but looked like he had to) I couldn't face any more of it.

John phoned me later that day.

I'm not sure how I can face telling you this.

I had not ruptured the water tank. What I had actually done was during one of my particularly profound crash mooring attempts, was I had ripped the overflow right off the side of the bow. Didn't even know I had an overflow. When the water tank was full, it carried on going filling the boat up too. I was scuttling my own boat. A bit embarrassing, that one.

There's more. I might as well get it all out. Turns out I had only very fractionally turned the water stop cock on. So when the boat was out of kilter (it happens a lot. You only have to put a week's worth of cider on one side and she lists like she's got a rugby team huddled together in a corner. Nothing to do with the sheer amount of cider, obvs), water was being directed away from the pump, causing it to kick in. Making it seem like I had a leak. Therefore it looked very much like I had escaped the worst possible leak ever scenario as well.

I bet you're wondering how I ever manage to put socks on in the morning (I don't).

CHAPTER 19

Early life

Eventually I did manage to find a house. I had trawled everywhere looking for the perfect little cottage to do up and flex my interior design muscles again on. This little cottage was tucked away down a track and was one of a terrace of industrial workers houses.

I had also opened my first shop at this point, selling reproduction pine furniture* and decorative interior solutions. The latter of which I practiced with alacrity on the interior of my new home. I cut massive stencils out, inspired by scribbles in my sketch book. I experimented by mixing all sorts of colours from my college acrylic paint box. I developed new furniture painting skills.

All this was trial and error. Mostly error it has to be said, but still I persevered.

Reproduction pine furniture was just starting to become popular. Mainly imported from Yugoslavia, a spin off from the period pine furniture that I had been stripping back in 1984.

The shop began really well. The repro pine market was booming. Which was just as well as the mortgage interest repayment rate in 1989 was 14.8% !!

That rate along with Thatcher's Poll Tax was always going to put a strain on my finances.

It took me 2 years of graft and experimentation to complete my second house.

In fact it looked so good, so quirky with all the stencils I had applied to the walls, the colours and paint effects I had used, it was featured in 'House Beautiful'.

Woohoo! Am interior design guru! I felt a victory dance and crowd surf was in order.

However, a couple of photos in a magazine was never going to pay the bills, the mortgage. The shop was floundering and the bills were mounting. I had to close the shop and sell my van to pay the overdue rates on it, so no victory dance and crowd surf for me then.

Except I did have a cunning plan hatching inside my tiny mind. Again.

As previously mentioned, my Mum and brother had set up an antique export business in Los Angeles, specifically Venice (beach). My brother Phil ran the shop out there and my Mum ran the shop at home. I had decided to rent the house out and go and live in Venice, California. I was hoping to get some furniture restoration work over there, piggy backed onto my brother's connections.

I hit a snag straight away with this great idea. I'd been in touch with the mortgage company who categorically stated that I was not allowed to rent my home out under the terms of their agreement.

Hmmmm...

Nothing Compares 2 U – Sinead O'Connor

Freedom! – George Michael

Everything I Do, I Do It for You – Bryan Adams

CHAPTER 20

ADVENTURES AT LAST

Awake My Soul – Mumford and Sons

Dream About Flying – Alexi Murdoch

Dear Friends - Elbow

With that drama out of the way and new guests in the house, I turned the boat round once again and headed north. Determined to get to the top of the British canal network. I also wanted to go down the Glasson arm of the Lanky into Glasson Basin where all the ocean going vessels were moored*

*Vessels from the Irish Sea can sail down the tidal River Lune, through a sea lock and moor in the basin

I was going to need help getting down the 6 big locks into the basin. With my dubious skill set and luck, the chance of catastrophe was high. Not least because if you left the lock gate paddles open all the way down you could actually drain the whole of the Lancaster canal into the Irish Sea! Can you imagine? The thought of it being me that drained the Lanky with my fuck-wittedness sent shivers down my spine.

I enlisted my good friend and fellow boater Jules to help. She was staying on the boat with me for 3 nights. My liver was going to have to cog up to Olympic function mode to get through it as we're buggers when we get together.

To have friends with me to enjoy these new experiences, really was what I had hoped boat life was going to be.

So on she jumped and off we went down the arm. Man alive it was beautiful. Like another world of nature. Boats only occasionally navigated this stretch so it felt completely untouched. The water was so deep and clear, shoals of fish, terrapins, water lilies, it was just lovely. There was nowhere to moor as the wild flowers covered both sides of the canal which although were visually stunning, it was also a little unnerving. My little boat was running warm to hot, especially in reverse (what was that about?) If anything went properly wrong I wouldn't be able to pull her in or pole her to the side as the water was so deep. I just had to brave it (again). Apart from that little stress it was a fabulous journey down culminating in the most humbling and overwhelming sight as we rounded the last bend.

Glasson Basin is massive, even making the huge ships, tugs and yachts look diminutive in the vast open water. My little boat looked like a match stick in comparison.

I had to navigate right across it in order to find the correct jetty that I'd booked for our 1 night stay whilst everyone on their boats reared up like meerkats watching, maybe even wishing for a catastrophe from me.

Do you know what though? I managed it. I found the right jetty and I moored up. A bloody miracle! There's nothing to see here suckers! Then tripped over a yacht's mooring lines getting off the boat I managed it. I found the right jetty and I moored up. A bloody miracle! There's nothing to see here suckers! Then tripped over a yacht's mooring lines getting off the boat.

The boat was actually too tiny for the jetty. My gunwales went beneath the jetty structure, too dangerous until I was given a couple of tyres to use as fenders on the jetty side. Now safely tied off, we left the boat and went out on a grand tour of Glasson (pub crawl) Of course we had a great night, so when 7am the next morning came and it was time to head back onto the Lanky, it was with a slightly jaded enthusiasm (some would call it a giant hangover) But we'd done it! We had navigated right down to the big sea lock where you could literally sail off into the North Atlantic Ocean, never to be seen again.

Next stop on the boat was Lancaster. My liver was already twitching in anticipation.

Lancaster was a blast, it was always going to be. Such a great city. I just love the fact that you can moor up free of charge in the heart of the city. It's just as well we were in the centre as by the time we'd fallen out of that pub with the band on and found a kebab shop we were well and truly lost. How can you lose a canal? But we did. It's not a good look to be staggering around a city of such profound architectural beauty with a kebab in one hand asking where you left your home on the canal. At least I knew that if I got on the towpath I just had to walk down it to eventually get to my boat.

That's why Jules and I are only allowed out for a maximum of 3 nights together. (But better than my bestie Jelly and I, who are only allowed a maximum of 1 night out together. I'm not going to make your hair curl with any of those stories, don't worry, I may however be unable to resist.)

Next day, Jules slept all the way back as I gingerly navigated the boat back to her car. Thank god for that, my liver announced.

CHAPTER 21

SWING BRIDGES AND SUNSHINE

We Haven't Turned Around – Gomez

Butterfly – Jason Mraz

Shine – Alexi Murdoch

I was beginning to run out of time. Last time I looked, I had months left to play with on this beautiful canal. I now had just over 2 weeks. John had fixed the overheating in reverse problem and although the boat was still running warm, I headed towards Tewitfield, the top of the canal. Third time lucky.

It all went pretty smoothly until I got to that swing bridge*. The only swing bridge on the Lanky.

*Swing bridges are dreaded by the solo boater. They are a massive design flaw. Essentially you moor up on the bridge landing, walk across the bridge and open it. Works perfectly well if there's 2 of you. Boat sails through, pulls in on the other side, second person closes bridge, gets back on the boat. Easy.

Solo, you pull the boat in to the bridge landing, walk across the bridge, open it and then you're stuck. Can't get back to the boat! How mental is that design?

I took advice. Every single boater I have ever met will give you advice on how to open a swing bridge. It goes from wait till someone comes along to help (could take days), to moor on the other side and open it (can't get in, too shallow, too many weeds / bushes), or get the boat up to the bridge and tie the bow rope to the bridge, open it then pull the boat up to you, get on and move the boat (crash into bridge potential extremely likely)

I ended up going for the 'take a good run at the closed bridge and twat it as hard as you can to open it' Leaving the boat moored up and me running at the bridge from the towpath.

What could possibly go wrong with that genius idea?

Everything went wrong with that genius idea.

First of all the bridge only swung open halfway so I couldn't get the boat through but also couldn't get the bridge back. Great. This is when the hecklers, I mean walkers, started going past. They couldn't help as the bridge was offside, but they did all stop to watch. I even think someone pulled out their sandwiches to kick back with and enjoy the show. I got back on the boat and slowly inched the bow of the boat as close as I could get to the bridge. As my boat is so tiny the bow could easily get stuck underneath the bridge so I had to go carefully. Then I skittered along the gunwales, got on the bow and did a kind of contorted mad climb to get on the bridge (I'm used to being up scaffolding with my work so for once my skill set came in handy) once on the bridge I tied the boat to it and went to open the bridge. The bloody boat started going sideways and was about to broadside the bridge in slow motion as I opened it. I had to reverse the contorted climb back onto the boat amidst well meaning but useless heckling from the now sizeable crowd that had formed and push the boat off the side of the bridge. I had to do this 3 sodding times in order to get enough space to get the boat through. At least the crowd were impressed with the show.

Thankfully the rest of the journey was lovely. Which was a blessed relief, I needed a break from all the stress and dramas I'd been having. It was really rural up there, loads of coots, moorhens and swans all with babies dipping in and out of the reeds. It looked more like a river than a canal. I went down the tiny Capernwray arm, the water of which was covered in duckweed the exact same colour as the exterior of the boat. It felt like I'd entered an Amazonian tributary. Another reason I love boating so much. The unexpected.

I eventually made it to Tewitfield, at last, third time lucky. I had wanted to spend time up there and walk the 14 miles of disused canal further on, but my time was running out, I needed to get back to the moorings. The boat was still running warm and I would have to get her fixed before the Ribble Link crossing.

There were also a few more places I'd like to go that were downstream on the Lanky. One particular place that I'd been to years previously had stuck in my mind even before I got involved with narrowboats. An eccentric jumble of shops, restaurants, a hotel and pub right on the canal side. Guys Thatched Hamlet.

A couple of days later after I'd flipped the house again for new guests (I had now accidentally diversified and become a cleaner. Man alive the pube factor in the cleaning up is massive) I jumped back on the boat. I'd had yet another spat with my disgruntled boyfriend, apparently I was a shit girlfriend that he couldn't keep track of. Fair point to be honest.

The UK was going through a melting heatwave and I couldn't think of anywhere nicer to be than cruising down the cut with my stupid mate Monkey.

John hadn't had time to fix the overheating problem which seemed to be something to do with the raw water pump getting blocked Also the starter battery, was playing up for some unfathomable reason as it had only just been replaced, along with the belts and alternator. So I'd had to borrow some jump leads and jump the starter battery from the leisure batteries to boot her up. I was still willing to risk another trip out though and here's me calling Monkey stupid.

CHAPTER 22

STUPID FRIENDS

Sally Cinnamon – The Stone Roses

LIFEGOESON – Noah and the Whale

Oh My God – Kaiser Chiefs

I set off from the moorings in 42 degree heat after getting the boat as cool as possible with all the doors and windows open and ice cream in the freezer. I managed to get, let's see, half a mile? before the boat had completely overheated and I had to pull in. Great. I bashed a pin in, moored up and called John.

The hottest day of what felt like the century and Big John was squashed in the hot engine bay dismantling my raw water pump that had detritus stuck in it.

God I felt so guilty, all I could do was feed him the ice cream to try and cool him down.

He managed it though and a couple of hours later I was up and running and heading down to Garstang to pick Monkey up with his ubiquitous carrier bag of Skol.

We had a lovely if horse fly bombarded cruise to Guys. I needed to turn the boat around before I moored as I was still nervous about jumping the batteries which was what I would have to do later, possibly (definitely) pissed. But the winding hole was an hour's return journey downstream, which I was all set for, however Monkey talked me in to turning on a 'wider bit' of canal. A manoeuvre I was extremely dubious about as I didn't want more crud getting stuck in my pump.

Guess what? I did exactly what he told me to do (I never listen to Monkey and there's a reason for that) I turned the boat into what turned out to be a mud slick and she immediately and fully overheated. Crud had indeed got stuck in the pump. Except this time there was nowhere to pull in. I had to cut the engine and let her slow motion crash into the bushes. Again. Monkey got the pole from the roof and started poling her towards a possible clearing in the weeds where we could jump off and pull her along to Guys. A bit like dragging a recalcitrant puppy along by it's lead. Guys was only round the corner so how difficult could it be?

Very difficult. That paired with a calamitous fuck up made for at least an hours pulling, wading, poling, swearing and laughing. I could have turned the boat round quicker in the winding hole and still had a fully functioning pump, but it wouldn't have been as hilarious as this mess was.

Anyway, we poled her into a small clearing, both got off to pull her along and hit a giant oversight pretty quickly. The boat managed to get jammed in a massive clump of weeds a good way from the tow path. So now there's no one on board, no means of freeing the boat and no way of climbing back on. Brilliant, a total pair of genius's right there. There was only one thing for it. I had to disrobe and wade in, get on the boat and get back to poling her gondola style again.

Can you imagine the scene? On the hottest day of the century at the most popular pub on the whole of the Lancaster canal. We poled the boat to a halt right outside, right next to the packed beer garden, alarmingly similar to Jack Sparrow in Pirates of the Caribbean when he steps off his almost completely sunk boat and onto the jetty. We honestly couldn't have looked more uncool and inept if we had tried. I think we only managed 2 pints before Monkey went home. Best 2 pints we ever had though.

So there I was, on the back deck of my boat. Pram cover up on beer garden side for privacy. Looking out over the water. On my broken down boat. Relationship in tatters.

I couldn't have been happier.

Something was happening to my soul. Something was unblocking in my heart.

CHAPTER 23

SEPARATION ANXIETY

Sweet Caroline – Neil Diamond

I Predict a Riot – Kaiser Chiefs

Don't Leave - Faithless

Time was now upon us and Monkey was starting to get separation anxiety.

We had one more opportunity for a night out together before I permanently set off south, for the trepidatious journey across the Ribble Link.

Our intention was to enjoy an evening listening to a fellow boater sing in the local bar, but it quickly got out of hand as we decided to splinter off. I really wanted to watch the sun set one last time at my favourite mooring half an hour's sail away at the Lambing Fields.

John had just completed the task of replacing the 51 year old pump and putting a giant basket filter on that should prevent all the overheating grief from happening again. The starter battery was a bit more of a conundrum though. I'd still have to give the old girl a jump start to get going for our last sail together, which was a miracle I managed to achieve. I was beginning to feel like I could cope with the idiosyncrasies (let's call them that instead of myriad of sodding breakdowns) of my boat. I was starting to learn to be an actual boater it seems. Not a moment too soon for all concerned.

We set off, Neil Diamond blasting out of the speaker, back to our true uncool selves, back on that beautiful little boat that was starting to feel like a sanctuary for me.

God 'Sweet Caroline' sounded so good that night (not the next day so much when sobriety hit it has to be said). I slowed the boat right down so we could enjoy more singing and dancing and laughing. Our last evening together on the boat. We'd had such a fantastic summer. Talking rubbish for hours. Watching sun sets, sat on the back deck under a teal blanket, just the best of mates.

I managed to moor up next to another boat with grace and aplomb (well it felt like that). Then decided to light a bonfire on the towpath in the collapsible fire pit I kept in the bow well, to keep us warm as darkness fell. We had been 'quietly' singing, sniggering and shushing so as not to disturb my neighbour when I went in for yet another glass of wine.

I'm not really sure how I managed it, but as I stepped off the boat in my bare feet (I'd spent all summer running about bare footed) I staggered, booted the fire pit which fell over, immediately setting the towpath and the teal blanket alight with a mighty Whumph! Oh my god, panic!

Monkey impulsively tipped his precious cans of Skol on the fire to quench the flames. No idea why, as there was a canal full of water right there.

Apparently, so Andrea on the next boat said the morning after, as she perused the damage that could only have been made by 50 people at a rave, we sounded like a pair of hysterically cackling and drunk ferrets running about trying to put out the flames. A miracle we didn't burn ourselves. Teal blanket didn't look too good though.

That began another friendship. I was to meet Andrea again on our travels over the Ribble Link and beyond. Another great positive that comes with living on the cut. The fortuitous meetings.

That said, it was probably a good time to get going. If Monkey and I spent anymore time together we'd have both ended up with ASBO's.

CHAPTER 24

Early Life

I'm not proud to tell you this but being told by most people I am not allowed to do something, never goes down well with me, never has either. Being told by a mortgage company I'm not allowed to do something was bound to make me kick a table over and flick the 'V's.

It didn't take me long to find a couple to rent the house. In retrospect maybe I should have vetted them a bit closer, but hey, what could possibly go wrong?

I put my springer spaniel sidekick, Joe Bell into kennels. Another slight gamble.

I've not troubled you with stories about my dog Joe Bell, he's a book in itself (I had only just retrieved him from Carlisle where he'd got a good 30 miles away from the site I was working on. Some kind soul found him wandering, took him in, renamed him 'Scamp' and it was only that I was listening to the local radio station that put a shout out about this poor lost doggy that I knew it was him. It was his modus operandi, the little sod. Don't get me started on Joe Bell.)

I'd booked my ticket to LA, nearly missed the plane as the bus I had brilliantly decided to catch to London was horribly delayed, but eventually managed to humph down in my seat at the back of the plane. Right next to a roadie for James Taylor.

In those days on long haul flights they gave you packs of 5 Dunhill's to smoke free of charge! (How mental is that?) and beer and wine and champagne, we ended up having a full smoking, boozing and snogging party on the back row.

Oof, this certainly boded well for my new Californian life.

(God I miss those days, the days before Tinder.)

I couldn't honestly say that I nested in the time I spent living in Venice, California.

I was living with my brother and 4 roofers from the UK and all sneakily working for cash. I had a great time though, it has to be said. My heart did begin yearning for nesting. Back home. I had quietly begun to realise I couldn't be too far away from my family and Jelly. I loved them too much and missed them too much. It just wasn't the same taking the piss out of Jel from so far away.

Through Phil's contacts and my networking I started restoring antiques, retouching paintings and furniture, gilding, graining and marbling. The antiques were imported from Italy and France, all slightly damaged in transit and all destined for a very swanky antique shop in Beverly Hills.

So I was expanding my skill spectrum and also erm my social spectrum it seemed.

I phoned Jelly every Saturday during this time. Didn't have one conversation with her when she was sober for 8 months. The time difference meant it was always her Saturday night. But she did keep me up to date with the chaos that was beginning to unravel.

Joe Bell had done a full jail break and been off chasing sheep (oh god). The smoke alarms had been constantly set off in the house by the tenants (again, oh god) but apart from that, everything was fine (she'd omitted the bit about the dog being shot at by the farmer, she reasoned because the farmer had missed, I didn't need to know this nugget of alarm – wise move)

I went back to being in denial and having a great time.

Until April 29th, 1992. When 4 policemen were acquitted of the savage beating of an unarmed black man, Rodney King. Then the shit really hit the fan, especially when a videotape of the incident hit television screens.

The riots lasted 6 days. In those 6 days I was taught how to load and fire a hand gun. Against my will it has to be said, but the lads I lived with were worried about me being very white and very alone in the house when they were working.

We lived in a predominantly black neighbourhood. All around the house were gunshots, fires, sirens and helicopter searchlights from all the break-ins and looting. I watched gangs of men walking down the middle of our street holding AK47's as if in a Rambo film. I just kept my head down until I could leave the house in the mornings to collect work and provisions. It seemed to me the best time to get out as all the baddies had knackered themselves out by then and gone to bed.

It might be time to think about coming home though, I reasoned.

Barely Afloat – Mostly Adrift – Always Laughing

Breaking the Girl – Red Hot Chilli Peppers

Let Love Rule – Lenny Kravitz

Lithium – Nirvana

CHAPTER 25

WACKY RACES

Going Down – Fun Loving Criminals

Walk On the Wild Side - Lou Reed

Leaders of the Free World - Elbow

It was indeed a weedy schlep to get to the spot where Huffler my tow boat was moored. I could now begin to understand why it was only the intrepid that would cruise this far south for fun. My little boat didn't have the power to move forwards with so much weed tangled around the propellor so I was having to stop every few minutes and get in the weed hatch (note to self every time I went in the hatch: put the lid back on firmly. The fastest way to sink a boat is through a leaky weed hatch and it's exactly the sort of thing I'd be likely to do)

It was the last night on the Lanky and time for number 1 crew member Kitty to jump onboard. We're peas in a pod Kitty and I so we had a great night on the back deck drinking cider, singing songs, laughing. A perfect last night.

I only realised the slight oversight after Kit had fallen asleep in my bed (I was sleeping on the sofa bed so I could get up early and move the boat to the first lock) Two girls can fill a toilet cassette up in one evening (stop looking so bloody smug, you men.) I couldn't swop the cassette for an empty one as it was under the bed where Kit was asleep. So by first light the next morning I was desperate for a wee.

I'm not sure what possibly made me think it was a good idea, but taking a saucepan out onto the open back deck and weeing in it seemed pretty straightforward at the time. So what are the chances of a stealth dog walker and his silent dog going past at exactly mid wee? Poor man. Poor dog too, come to that.

It took an hour sailing, stopping, de-weeding and sailing to reach Savick Brook Basin.

There were 8 boats in total crossing the Link on that hottest of August days. We all paired up to reverse into the first staircase lock*. However, I lost my nerve with reversing so jumped off and uncoolly dragged the boat into the lock with my stern line. I'd had enough humiliation already that day and it was only 8am.

*A staircase flight of locks is an incredible feat of engineering. As you come down the first lock, the gates open and you immediately pull into another lock, and so on. Just like a set of stairs. It's unnerving if you're going down a big staircase flight as you can't see what's ahead of you. It feels like you're going to tip off the end of a precipice. I suppose reversing down these had it's merits, although it's still an extremely odd feeling.

Huffler and I duly reversed down the staircase. Sailing out, we turned the boats forwards and suddenly found ourselves in the most bewitching stretch of water. This really was a brook! The trees had grown over the brook on both sides creating an Amazonian tunnel for us to travel through. Both boats struggled with the shallow water, constantly running aground but the experience was so incredibly worth it. We'd found ourselves in what felt like a forgotten, secret paradise.

All the boats eventually moored at the big sea lock with trepidation, where we would wait for the tide to be at it's highest point enabling us to cross in a flotilla.

I could not leave the tiller for one moment on the 3 hour crossing so I had to make sure my crew of 2 and I were lifejacketed up, 2 way radios working to keep in touch with Huffler

There's a strict time limit to get across the 4 mile tidal stretch as you don't want the tide turning and going out, taking your boat out to sea with it. Then there are the rip tides that can throw you totally off course and onto the many hidden sand banks.

There's the wind factor too. Narrowboats are keel-less so can easily be blown off course, or even roll. Thank god I was being towed. I was sailing under my own steam and was only being led, but without my tether I could easily find myself stranded on a sandbank overnight, waving at a BBC news crew.

Picture the scene, 8 boats all tightly breasted up to each other on the holding jetty, bobbing around side by side, like whippets in a trap. Engines are already over heating, so are the skippers. The lock keeper appears on the horizon and gives the thumbs up.

And we're off!!

It was like Wacky Races! Everyone's vying to be first through the lock, no time to waste. The boats are bumping off each other as we all barrel out of the sea lock, go round a bend to then enter the Ribble estuary. As we did this we could see the rip tides we were just about to hit - swirling, fast, angry stretches of water to be navigated around. We had all started in a huddle, now all 8 boats were scattered right across the open water. Some clearly struggling and careening around, others picking their way through, some charging along with powerful engines.

It was truly magnificent. To be sailing out on open water, the vast expanse of sea and sky was incredibly overwhelming especially having been hidden in a what felt like an Amazonian tributary only minutes before.

Tony and Margaret on Huffler were superb, the crossing was going smoothly. I started to relax.

Then I hit a rip tide that Tony had managed to dodge and the boat started acting like a water ski, swerving dramatically from side to side, the waves splashing up the gunwales, being pulled forwards by a rope that looked like it could snap at any moment under the force. It was a massive struggle to correct her even under my own power and being towed, she hit sand bank after sand bank, listing wildly. I was truly amazed that Tony could navigate so accurately through the undeniably treacherous waters. He pulled me through on what undoubtedly, because of the profound and fast tidal change, would have been an overnight stay on a sand bank in the middle of the Ribble Estuary for me, the boat and my crew (on reflection at that moment, having precious cargo on board in the form of my daughter was a tad rash). That, or my little boat would have been out to sea, backwards and upside down without my tether.

It was a harsh and absolute education of how wrong things could go in the blink of an eye and a note to myself not to relax too much again.

A little while after this, as I was enjoying watching all the different sea birds flying over and admiring the wild washing machines and ubiquitous shopping trolleys beached on the river banks, I saw something on the horizon. It was getting closer quickly. A tug boat. Okay, what was this about then?

He got intimidatingly right along side us and asked which boat was in distress (clearly he thought it was me as he'd been watching me swing like a pendulum off the back of Huffler).

Ooh! A boat in distress though! I'd been too busy water skiing to notice. Apparently one of the boats was over heating, having to fight themselves out of a riptide that required full engine revs to try and stop them going sideways, then backwards. They were well off piste and behind schedule so made the emergency call for a tow. How exciting! – that it wasn't me.

It took 9 hours total sailing to get from the mooring that morning (where I'd had my embarrassing wee that now seemed weeks ago) to moor up in Tarleton, a branch of the Leeds and Liverpool canal and onto the main waterways network where I could virtually go anywhere.

I was profoundly knackered, blissfully joyful and really quite proud of myself.

The journey that I had just completed had been a cause of much anxiety and restless nights.

And now look at me! Moored in a long line of fellow boats having all crossed together. I really did feel like a proper boater.

Now the adventures could really begin!

ADRIFT PART 2

CHAPTER 26

Early Life

I really needed to be married, I'd decided. (I'd had an attempt at talking a previous boyfriend round to marrying in Vegas then getting divorced the day after in Tahoe, but strangely he wasn't up for it)

I obviously had to take this task a bit more seriously. Now then, who to marry? Tricky.

I was back home from L.A., reunited with my bad dog Joe and my trashed and slightly charred 'House Beautiful' home.

I'd been back working and painting a kitchen where a cabinet maker was working.

Well, I had no idea that he was the first boy I'd ever kissed at 13. I'd still got the tapes he'd recorded for me back then, mostly sellotaped back together after being chewed up in my Sanyo cassette player.

It was quite a shock that he gave me this information over a pint a couple of weeks later.

Turns out our paths had crossed quite often (no wonder I couldn't find a husband, I was completely oblivious and utterly useless in the romance department. Obvs)

Anyway. Apparently a few weeks after this revelation, after a Big Night Out, I asked him to marry me (full disclosure, I still don't remember to this day ever asking him)

To kind of retrieve what romance I could out of my amnesia, I suggested we get married on the beach in California. This brainwave was barely 6 months after the Rodney King riots.

To be fair, although it was a whirlwind romance, we did fall in love and our businesses complimented each other's which meant we could work together also. So off we flew back to Venice Beach, California, 3 months after we had re-met on that kitchen.

It was a simple hippy wedding on the beach at sunset. My LA friends came as did a couple of relatives. We afforded 1 bottle of champagne which we opened after the ceremony and drank right there on the beach.

Then the police came and arrested us.

Apparently it's illegal to drink alcohol on the beach. What the hell? That's what beaches are designed for, surely? Not in the States they're not. Bloody Americans.

We got a 'get out of jail free' card the same evening, completely lost the marriage certificate never to be seen again and partied hard till dawn.

The next day and still slightly hungover with only $8 left to our names we took the mile or so stroll to Phil's antique shop from the house. A walk I'd done many times on my own.

Suddenly we heard the footsteps of about 6 people approaching quickly behind us. Before we had time to react, my brand new husband was hit over the head and dropped to the floor. Two of the black lads restrained me whilst the other four took it in turns to run and jump with both feet on my husband's head. How it didn't burst like a balloon I have no idea. They robbed all $8 from us and legged it after fully kicking the shit out of him. I honestly thought he was dead. I could not compute what had happened.

Apparently it was quite straight forward, said the police whilst the ambulance whipped my non insured husband to the hospital for an emergency MRI scan. These young black lads just wanted to kick 'whitey'. It was too close to the Rodney King affair not to still have tensions between black and whites running high.

More to the point the policeman added, they were just little twats using a racial excuse to beat and rob.

We ran up $25000 worth of hospital bills in 12 hours.

With my brand new husband battered and concussed and me pale and shaky with shock, we jumped on a plane the next day, never to return.

'Paranoid' Black Sabbath – from me to him on our wedding day.

'Baker Street' Gerry Rafferty — from him to me on our wedding day.

"Sweet Home Alabama' Lynyrd Skynyrd — first dance, that everyone danced to.

All taken from that tape he made me 13 years previously.

CHAPTER 27

HOME WATERS

On & On – Longpigs

Windows Are Rolled Down – Amos Lee

In A State – UNKLE

I was in my longed for home waters now. Very exciting. Now that the drama of crossing the link was behind me I could enjoy the sail up the hefty locks of the Rufford Branch and onto the Leeds and Liverpool canal proper. It took a day of victory sailing with Jelly, Jules and Kitty on board, all my faves who had been through so much with me on my journey so far, to get to my home town of Parbold. This was the bit I'd dreamed of. I had lived near the canal in Parbold for many years, my mum opened her first antique shop right next to the then working grain mill on the cut. In those days the canals were horrendous. Full of rusty bikes, dead dogs and choked with weed. No one in their right mind used the canals in those days for leisure, the rats the size of cats were enough to put you off, never mind the rest of the horrors.

But now, 50 years on, this canal held all the charm, solace and adventure I had longed for. This was the bit when I brought my precious boat home. The bit that I'd focussed on through the dark and difficult days.

On mooring up and relishing it, the girls and I did a magnificent crowd surfing loop of all the pubs in the village, just like I'd promised myself.

Disgruntled boyfriend who had kicked off so much with me constantly being MIA on the boat, gave a huge sigh of relief. At least I was going to be at home now that I had the boat back. He'd have a sensible, well behaved girlfriend that wore shoes from now on.

I had a wonderful time taking friends and family out on little cruises now that I was so close to home.

A notable one was taking my sister and niece out for the day. It was a glorious day. Last time my sister was on a boat was her wedding day and we spent a lovely while reminiscing and telling her daughter about it. After our picnic towpath side and on return, just as I was about to moor up back home, the engine alarmingly overheated. Again. I tried the old butter knife trick. This time I took the sea cock hose off and blew into it to try and remove the blockage from the inlet pipe. Get me being a boat mechanic! (Full disclosure, I had Big John on a video call showing me how to do it) The pipe was too blocked, it wouldn't shift. What I needed was some Big Equipment. I needed an air hose. Not the easiest thing to find on a towpath. Also I'd have to plug it in somewhere. Now how the hell was I going to achieve this? Can't move the boat as she's overheating. Can't start the engine to power the air hose because she's overheating and there is no other 240v supply available. Hmmm

Miraculously I found a portable air hose (not very portable as it was heavy as hell) and a couple of extension reels. Next was to charm my one and only boat neighbour to move their boat next to mine and leave their engine running so I could use their mains power. That way I could fire up the compressor and shoot air through the hose to unblock it.

Guess What? It only went and worked! A jubilant wriggle dance on the towpath followed. I'd actually fixed her! Thanks again to getting unconditional help from a fellow boater. I so love the cut for this.

Once home and after the busy days flipping the house for yet more guests, and the busy days boat tripping my family and friends, I began to reminisce about my time on the Lanky. Although I'd had friends joining me occasionally, I had predominantly been on my own. I was beginning to realise that I liked my solitary adventures. I couldn't put my finger on it, but something was creeping into my soul. Something was beginning to heal.

I was desperate to set off on a bigger solo adventure, back to my solitary boat life and the feelings of completeness that were beginning to nudge in on me. I'd no idea where to at that stage, the only thing I knew was I was going to have to learn a lot and quickly about single handing through locks, swing-bridges and tunnels. Eek. And navigating, booking passage through specific locks and timings! How the hell was I supposed to know how long it took travelling? There were a myriad of questions going through my mind. Where could I moor safely as a lone female? It's not like a camper that you can just drive away quickly if there's trouble. At night I was locked in the boat, I couldn't go anywhere, so I really did have to be careful. Maybe some careful planning would be prudent at this stage.

CHAPTER 28

GOING SOLO

Moving – Supergrass

You Could Be Happy – Snow Patrol

Ruby – Kaiser Chiefs

Sod it. I decided to just set off and hope for the best.

The first hurdle was getting through the Deep Lock. No one in their right mind single hands through the dreaded Deep Lock and I wasn't about to either. Cue facebook. I put a shout out for help. Help came in the form of a lovely young solo boater who brought me gently up through the terrifying Deep Lock and through the next lock, 2 miles further on. Where he left me, walking the whole way back to his boat. How lovely is that? Someone will take the time and effort to help a complete stranger out. Boating life, it's a different kind of life entirely and one I was completely besotted with.

That was day 1 of my new adventure. It was also day 1 of being single as disgruntled boyfriend totally spat his dummy out and chucked me. No matter. I was used to it, being a fully fledged rubbish girlfriend and all.

I moored up for the night. My idea was to try and find another boat to buddy up through the next load of locks with. Except there was no one, not one single boat moving. Bugger. I dawdled the next day not having the courage to set off when at last a boat went passed and yes! I could join him. He'd even set the lock and wait for me so I could just sail straight in! (Didn't have the heart to tell him that me sailing straight in anywhere had never happened yet, he'd have to find out the hard way.)

There began another friendship with my boat buddy Paul, another fortuitous meeting and what was to become a crash course (literally) in single handing and navigating.

Things were looking up. I had also been reinstated as a girlfriend again, albeit a shit one apparently. Whatevs.

Next stop was mooring next to Andrea (my tolerant neighbour from the torched towpath on the Lanky). She was trying to get to her home moorings but was stuck due to low water levels, it happens a lot in summer, just another conundrum to get round (If you ask a boater where they're heading, most will say 'no idea' as plans often change because of stoppages. But I love this. No fixed abode. No fixed plans. You can see why I'm considered a shit girlfriend then.)

We went wild swimming*. Wild swimming! I'd never been wild swimming before. I love this too. Other's random hobbies that you get to join in on. We barbecued and bonfired and drank red wine. Then Andrea leapt up. She'd seen an otter! Oh my god, an otter! Giant swimming rat more like. Time to call it a night I think. Monkey was jumping on the boat the next day to sail into Manchester (somewhere he'd never been! He only lives an hour away from Manchester!!) so god knows what was going to unravel with that one.

*No one ever, ever goes swimming in the canal. We all know what's in there. If a boater accidentally falls in they look traumatised for at least a week thinking they're going to come down with Weil's disease, a disease contracted from rat urine and contaminated water – for the record I have never fallen in. Yet. But it's only a matter of time.

Next day Monkey duly jumped on the boat and the boat immediately broke down. Knew I should have called him Jonah. I got my butter knife out again and after a couple of unintentional donuts, we set off again, Manchester bound. Something I had always wanted to do was sail my own boat into Manchester.

Man alive, it was everything I'd hoped it would be. I was moored in the heart of cosmopolitan Manchester, in Castlefield free of charge for 2 nights. Ooh let's get dressed up, go out and drink glamorous cocktails! Except oh my god, it was like dragging Crocodile Dundee around the city with me. Monkey, not used to tall buildings, cars or people and only used to drinking cans of Skol was a bit perplexed by it all. To counteract his indecision I got a 2p piece out and flipped it at every venue we came across. Heads you walk on, tails you go in and get a drink. We even managed to blag it right up to the roof terrace of The Ivy.

You should have seen Monkey's face! He got the hang of it after about 11 cocktails. Then it was decided to go down Canal Street, part of Manchester's Gay Village. Pride was on and the place was bouncing. Well I've never seen a person more delighted, more at home and loving it more than Monkey at Pride!! Makes sense really, I'd been witness to his dancing many times so had an inkling.

The next day I left Monkey watching the Pride procession with his eyeballs on sticks and his tongue hanging out. I had bigger fish to fry. I was meeting up with coifed disgruntled boyfriend and his swanky mates. When you've been running around with no shoes on, jumping in lakes and laughing at water rat sightings it's a pretty big ask to tidy yourself up enough to look respectable and go out with civilised people. In fairness we had a great night. I now had a happy boyfriend! Yay! Wonder how long that will last.

CHAPTER 29

Early Life

I had sold my house so now my husband and I had nowhere to live. We decided to camp out in his parents' decrepit barn. It was a shithole, was coming into winter and was bloody freezing. I threw myself into making what I could out of it. Whilst I was on with polishing this particular turd, the new husband 'wired up' the electric shower by putting a 13 amp socket on the end of it and asked me to jump in and try it.

Bang! The whole thing exploded.

It was the middle of winter. I was living in a freezing earwig infested barn with an outside toilet and a husband that was trying to electrocute me.

This did not bode well for a new marriage.

Around this time my client's were holding a Christmas party. I definitely had to crash it. It was being held in the Banqueting Hall where I had spent months restoring the oak panelling and ageing the reproduction Gothic strapwork plaster ceiling.

As I skulked in trying to look like I was supposed to be there, I was approached by a gentleman. Bugger, I'd been busted I thought. Instead though, he began chatting to me. He asked if I had done the ceiling in the Hall to which I confirmed I had. Would you like to do mine? Came the question. Yeah, go on then, I replied.

Turns out that gentleman was Sir Peter Moores, third richest man in the country at that time. There began a long friendship and an 18 year rolling contract restoring, decorating and designing the interiors of Parbold Hall, his home.

Why he chose me instead of top-endy architects and designers was beyond me at that stage. It was only later that I realised he'd trust a problem solving, back chatting, wild card over any coifed 'yes' man, any day.

I was given some amazing commissions from him. Some were totally bat shit, others were very privileged.

One time he'd decided he didn't like the background colour of his Music Room carpets. Could I change the background colour from cream to pink? Erm, yeah?

Jelly ended up doing this vicariously with me as it was so boring crawling around on a floor staining minute areas between the patterns, pink, for weeks and weeks on end that I couldn't stop texting her, baiting her and taking the piss out of her. Jelly for brains, you see.

I know I'm going off piste here but there was this time she'd just been given some Pink Fir Apple potatoes which perplexed her. She text me, should she peel the fur off them first to eat them?

Another day or so later I text her saying I'd been given a stool that had so much woodworm in it, the worms were almost holding hands.

'Is that what they do then, woodworms hold hands?'

Time past quickly when you had Jelly as a friend.

Husband, bad dog Joe Bell and I managed 2 years camping in that miserable barn.

We had enough money now thanks to Sir Peter to set up our first interiors shop together and find a do-upper house to buy and live in. Another bloody camping experience was on the cards, however I wasn't about to get in any more showers he'd rigged for me again, that was for sure.

All I Wanna Do – Sheryl Crow

Ironic – Alanis Morissette

Kiss From a Rose – Seal

CHAPTER 30

CANAL CARNAGE

Wonderwall – Oasis

My Sad Captain – Elbow

Have A Nice Day – Stereophonics

I left Manchester feeling pretty good. A happy boyfriend and my mate Monkey on the verge of a sexual revelation. Well, as close as he could get to one which wasn't really that close at all, in all honesty.

I set sail for Dunham Massey. Now then, this is an absolute peach of a place to moor up. Dunham Massey is a National Trust house with a deer park full of fallow deer. The best time to see them is at dusk when everyone's gone home and they come out of the shadows to eat and play. All it takes is jumping a fence to get in! (Don't tell anyone)

I'd promised Jelly this trip into the park and was a little trepidatious as she's a cross between a baby giraffe and a wrecking ball, a dead cert to scare deer away, that and the fact that her bag was clunking with cider...

It was actually breathtaking in the park that evening. We sat down in a clearing, kicked back with a cider and waited. Then a stag sauntered out of the gloaming, stared majestically at us, then suddenly reared on his hind legs. He thrust his antlers into the branches of the oak tree he was standing under and shook the tree. We couldn't work it out at first, but then came to realise he was pulling the acorns down to eat! A truly magnificent sight to behold. In fact, he seemed a bit too regal to be hanging out with two cider swigging trespassers, if I'm honest.

That's yet another thing I love about boat life. It gives you the opportunity to slow down and witness these wonderful spectacles, even if you do have to jump a fence to do it!

It was now time to move into enemy territory. Anderton. All I had to do was blast through, at 3 miles an hour, get to Middlewich and out of ex-boyfriend's home waters. Easier said than done. First I had to navigate 3 tunnels single handed, something I was absolutely bricking it about.

I hit an all time record in nervy poos that morning I set off, easy double figures.

I was literally shitting it about these 3 timed tunnels. What if I got the timings wrong? What if I couldn't see? What if I got claustrophobia and panicked halfway through? Also it was changeover day at the boat hire companies which meant hire boaters careening wildly everywhere making for a total chaotic zoo.

I managed it though, in more of a contact sport way than skilfully navigated way.

I moored up after a long and traumatic day, in a heap, ready for yet another day's trauma which was going through the busy and gongoozely* Middlewich locks. This was only going to end in my profound humiliation. Guaranteed.

*No idea who came up with that mad name. A gongoozeler is a person watching boats and canal life go past them.

God I had no idea why I was putting myself through all this torture.

Enemy territory, tunnels, locks, a big boozed up audience at the pub directly next to the first big scary lock.

I pulled up, bracing myself for the humiliation, when I heard a familiar voice. My boat buddy Paul on his push bike. He knew I was feeling shredded and had biked down to help me. Bless him. He was moored further up ready for our tandem journey into Chester. Big relief and disaster averted.

We got to Chester in 2 days. A slight couple of dramas on the way (one I'm in a bit of denial about, so I may not mention it)

After the erm big drama, we got to yet another lock. This was a lock made oddly from iron. Apparently because of subsidence, they made an iron tank into a lock or something like that.

Paul's on the towpath, dropping the water out of the lock, I'm on the boat, his boat is unmanned next to me. No problem, we do this all the time these days (being cool single handed boaters, and all). He opens the gates, the one my boat is behind will only partially open. No problem, he only has to get on his boat and go out first then I'll follow. Turns out there's no ladder in this lock because of it being just an iron tank. We didn't even notice until it was too late. Paul couldn't get on his boat and mine was stuck behind the jammed lock gate. Shit. Now what to do? There will have been more reasoned and clever ways of solving this problem but my solution was ramming the bejesus out of his boat to move it forwards. It worked of a fashion too. My little boat booted his big boat out of the lock and crashed it into the towpath. Not the most graceful of manoeuvres.

At least I was using my crashing skills in a useful way for a change.

Okay. I'll tell you.

I really did want to glide smoothly over this episode, as it does seem like I sail into potential navigational issues entirely unprepared. There's no need to comment at this point, thank you.

This potential 'navigational issue' is affectionately called the 'Bunbury Shuffle'. It's even got a name, so there's a hint right away.

Basically, it's a staircase of locks with no gaps to manoeuvre if there are any boats already on the staircase coming the other way.

Imagine, if you will, a football team coming down your house stairs and another football team going up your house stairs at the same time. What happens next? Who wins?

Not me on this particular staircase, nor any of the boats around me, that's for sure.

The Bunbury Shuffle goes something like, you have to shuffle your boat sideways to allow the boat coming towards you, to fit snugly into the lock beside you.

Not the jam the lock with the entire length of your boat trauma that actually happened.

I panicked, you see. Paul had managed to get through earlier with no trouble and all the other lovely hire boaters had you-tubed themselves to death, so knew exactly what to expect. Full disclosure, I did try and do some homework beforehand, except all the searching I managed to get up on You Tube was porn. I'm not sure if it was my settings to blame or a slight misspelling of the word 'bunbury', but it distracted me enough not to go any further anyhow.

(I have since revisited YouTube and put the word 'bunbury' into the search bar. For investigational purposes only, I promise. It auto corrects to 'bumburp'. Which is actually fabulously appropriate for my experience with it. I did the Bumburp Shuffle!)

What ensued was canal carnage. Boats jammed, boats bashed and all of us stuck as the leaking lock we were in was slowly emptying as we were trying to disentangle ourselves from each other. Total humiliation on my part, couldn't even blame the lovely hire boaters (which is something every, and I mean every paid up boat owner does, usually with a 'those bloody hire boaters' pre fix to every sentence)

It took about 19 people all heaving ropes and opening gate paddles, nearly 2 hours of heft and swear words to fix my misdemeanour. You can understand why I didn't want to mention it.

CHAPTER 30

TV TRAUMA

Not A Job – Elbow

Aisha – Death In Vegas

Sideways – Citizen Cope

Anyway, moving swiftly on.

The medieval city of Chester was stunning. Mooring up right alongside the ancient city walls was magnificent. I spent luxury time walking along the tops of the walls and drinking in the fascinating history of the city.I love the fact that boat life enables you to slow down, submerse yourself in your surroundings, enjoy all it has to offer, rather than rush through at a pace of an expensive mini break's tick list.

I had to get going though. I had to leave Chester, as I had a date with a TV production company that had been in touch. They had seen my facebook postings on a few different pages. Just me being a boat idiot with my adventures and breakdowns mostly, but it turned out that's what interested them. They were making a pilot for a hopeful new series on Channel 4 and could they please film my activities?

We had agreed to meet at the bottom of a flight of locks that were at the mouth of the bewitching Llangollen canal. Somewhere I was desperate to go, I'd heard so many stories about it's beauty and the breathtaking highest canal aqueduct in the world.

Filming was actually great fun if a little chaotic, not necessarily down to the crew, mostly down to my boating skills. One particularly dramatic episode that stands out (indelibly engraved on my brain, more like) was when the cameraman beside me on the back deck was filming me navigating into a tight single lock. Not an easy thing to do for either of us as he was a big fella with a big camera and also slightly unsteady on his feet, having never filmed or even been on a narrowboat before. Basically, as we approached the bottom of the lock, he staggered to the side, grabbed the side rail to prevent himself falling in, missed and dislodged the canopy instead which then hung over the side of the boat making me too wide to fit in the lock. I grabbed him by the earphones and pulled him back in whilst trying to stop the boat, steer the boat and haul my brand new £3000 pram cover back into the boat. It was never going to go well.

The boat smacked into the side wall of the lock, bounced off, banged into the other side and kind of interference fitted herself with a few more bashes and scrapes into the bottom of the lock. A shocked cameraman was seen hoofing up the lock ladder, fast as humanly possible, desperate to put as much space between himself, me and my boat as possible.

That was the end of my chance of being the new Robbie Cummings then.

Mercifully, the return journey home from the mouth of the Llangollen was pretty mellow. The season had started to change, it was mid September and I found myself savouring every moment of these adventures. The leaves were turning to their autumnal colours, apples were bobbing past me as they fell from the trees and into the water. Hedges were laden with sloes, rose hips and crabapples. The smell of summer had been replaced by the earthy, subdued smells of early autumn.

I'd begun to assess, reminisce and wonder at the psychological change in me.

I had always chased love, companionship, the whole ideal. I think I'd been hooked on it. I do have a very addictive personality, after all. I honestly believe I could get addicted to anything. Jelly's the same. We spent a whole year collecting pebbles just to make mosaics with them, that's one of a hundred examples of obsessions we got addicted to together.

I think I'd been so addicted to the yearning of love, a boyfriend, companionship that I hadn't listened carefully enough to what I had actually wanted.

I did, however, know, I didn't want this adventure to be over, but I really did have to come home. Grasp the nettle. Paint. I'd got commissions stacking up and lord knows I needed the money.

Also, I was beginning to get a little worried about Jelly. She was falling over just a bit more than she ever used to. It was always difficult to tell as she was so cack handed and so cack footed. Hence the name 'Jelly'. It always amazed me why she chose being a sculptural ceramicist as her vocation. I was always listening to her saying she'd gone and snapped a dog's leg off, or bashed a pig's ear off. She was a rare and fabulously successful talent though, her sculptures were utterly beautiful.

CHAPTER 31

LIVERPOOL

Soul Singing – The Black Crowes

Orange Sky – Alexi Murdoch

Belter – Gerry Cinnamon

Well that lasted exactly 2 weeks.

2 weeks of being home, working, catching up with the kids and checking on Jel. Being a real and proper girlfriend. With shoes on.

Then an Indian Summer descended and I decided off the cuff to sail into Liverpool. A round trip of 56 miles, 12 locks and here's the bugger, 32 swing bridges.

Full disclosure. It did feel like I was pushing it a bit, I was worried about Jel, but it was nothing I could put my finger on and she hated fuss. So I decided to squeeze a last adventure in. I was obsessed with that little boat and couldn't bear to think that the season might be over. That I might have to tuck her up safely in a marina for winter.

Maybe should have mentioned it to disgruntled boyfriend before I set off though. He lost his shit with me when he found out. Oh well. I had been chucked more times than a ball thrown at a rugby match in the few halcyon months we had spent going out together. I figured I'd manage just fine without him.

Paul was out on his boat miles away and so this really was an entirely solo adventure. It works having a boat buddy, I've found. Although we only occasionally travelled and moored up next to each other, we both knew where each other was and often made plans to meet along the canal network.

Life can get quite solitary living on a boat. Sure, I could moor next to other boats and the romantic in me likes to think we could all buddy up and have towpath barbecues and swop stories. It's not really like that in reality. Life is not like that in reality, is it? So many people are lonely. I was lonely, even within my marriage. As you can tell though, I can be a bit blasé about it, especially regarding my disgruntled now ex-boyfriend. All I was doing was braving it, really.

Anyway loneliness never stopped me doing anything. I just kick my bravery in again and man alive I was going to need to for this new adventure. I was going into Bandit Country, where only the intrepid (read that as stupid) moor casually without research and forethought. There were also 16 swing bridges to get through. One a timed one because of the busy road the canal breaches across, many of the bridges were off-side and manual. My last solo swing bridge on the Lancaster canal still sent shivers down my spine, so god knows why I thought this trip was a good idea. There were also large areas where mooring was extremely ill-advised due to the rough neighbourhoods the canal traversed through. It's a tricky thing this. Cruising down the canal, it's really easy not to be aware of the surrounding environment. You can literally be in the moment of a serendipitous scene where Kingfishers are sword fighting for territory, and there can be a stabbing in the next street, where you didn't even know there was a street!

I had taken advice. I knew where I had to get to that was (relatively) safe mooring on the 3 day journey there. All I had to do was get to the chosen mooring spots before dark and as this was the end of September, my sailing hours were becoming limited, so I had to be expeditious with my sailing so as not to have to cruise in the dark, not something I had ever managed before, I hasten to add.

No one, apart from boaters with a love of night swimming whilst being shot at with air rifles, would ever sail at night through these waters. Indeed, passing the boats I came across that were not in a boat club flotilla or marina, had grilles on their windows, to prevent little scrotes shooting boat windows out from the comfort of their bedrooms.

I managed fine. In fact better than fine. It was incredibly knackering though.

The first night I moored rurally just after the farmer had sprayed his field with utterly noxious rotted fish manure. So that was me and every possible molecule of the boat stinking of rotting fish for the next 2 days, a turn off for most baddies and burglars right there.

I met some charming drug dealers (yes, really) who were happy to open the automatic swing bridges for me with my special waterways key (in fact one dealer was so delighted that I'd given him so much 'power' as he called it, he gave me a

£10 bag of weed, on the house. I could learn to love these people.) and who knew that the underbelly of the canal system had such customer service?

I successfully made it to Litherland secure moorings. Yes, secure! I was safely moored offside, in a locked compound behind Tesco. A fine place to watch nefarious and entertaining activities on the towpath proper, and very handy for cider purchases, which was just as well as a storm had descended leaving me stranded. Sailing into Liverpool was only navigable in relatively clement weather, any wind turbulence meant being thrown and pinned against the harbour wall, which was something I was keen to avoid (back to that waving at a BBC TV crew scenario again).

The sail into Liverpool was magnificent. I had been stuck in Litherland for 3 days until the storm past, but it was all worth it. Sid, the lock keeper helped me down the first lock flight, then I was off! I sailed past the largest brick building in the world, the Tobacco Warehouse, along a new cutting called 'Sid's Ditch', turns out my lock keeper was a celebrity hero who had dug the ditch allowing passage into the Liverpool docks 13 years previously, before that the canal was unnavigable. What a hero he was too! Sid's Ditch allowed me to sail right past the spectacular Liver Building with it's 18' tall Liver birds crowning the top, through the slightly overwhelming Albert Dock (note to self; do not go the wrong way and make a boat idiot out of myself in front of all the throngs of shoppers and diners) Finally mooring up in the massive Salthouse Dock, right in the heart of the city itself. Magnificent indeed!

I had a wonderful time taking the family out on the boat, eating in the restaurants at the dock that sunny Sunday I sailed in, it was like being on holiday and a bit of a dream come true. I had always wanted to do this. This is what had been driving me forwards on the dark, tear stained days and nights of restoring the boat.

CHAPTER 32

Early Life

The do-upper house we ended up buying was actually a bank! We bought a disused bank in a cute local village. The aim was to convert the upstairs into a large flat for us to live in and the banking hall into 2 flats that we could rent out. We secured a 'buy to let' mortgage, I did the design work, husband did the building work and my wages from the Parbold Hall commissions paid for it. Great teamwork right there.

I was back to nesting again. I wanted a baby. Desperately. It was time, I had waited 13 years for this time to come around, 13 years of tears and turmoil and striving to get to a point in my life when I felt secure enough financially and mentally to bring a baby into the world.

But it didn't happen.

No amount of trying made my baby. Years went by, tears went by, but still no baby. How could life be so unfair? I railed. I was medically intervened with, tests were made, medication given, therapy, I tried everything, yet no baby.

Eventually I decided to give myself a break, have some time off this anguish, go on holiday with perplexed husband. Enjoy ourselves instead of caning it with work and worry. And yes, you guessed it, I got pregnant! If I'd known it was only going to take 5 days in Cephalonia reading 'Captain Corelli's Mandolin', I'd have done it bloody years ago (except it had only just come out in paperback, so maybe not).

How did I think that now I was pregnant it was going to be easy? Man alive, from conception to birth it was traumatic. The first 14 weeks I spent in a threatened pregnancy, I nearly ran out of blood in that time until they operated on me to save the baby or lose it, the gamble was that high. Actually. I'll not bore you with it, we all have our stories to tell, but you get the picture.

Ted was born by emergency c-section after a 43 week pregnancy (felt more like a 43 year pregnancy to all concerned), I was left on the gurney, belly open, whilst the night team rushed off to another emergency. That's me with MRSA then, but who cares? Because I had my yearned for, cried for, begged for baby at long, long last held within my arms. And what a crumper he was! Two foot long, 9lb 6oz, masses of blond hair and as hungry as his dad. To me though, just looking at him felt like I was eating chocolate. To this day, every time I look at my gorgeous boy, it still feels like I'm eating chocolate.

Kiss From a Rose – Seal

Ocean Drive – Lighthouse Family

The Miseducation of Lauryn Hill – Lauryn Hill

CHAPTER 33

BOAT BASTARDS

Lochloosa – JJ Grey and Mofro

Falling Out Of Reach – Guillemots

Drive – Joe Bonamassa

I stayed moored in Salthouse Dock for exactly 20 whole hours.

There was another storm coming in, but I had a window of a couple of days to get home. There were two boats leaving that Monday morning and I'd asked if I could buddy up with them, I couldn't face doing all those swing bridges on my own again (and I didn't want to push it with the drug dealers I'd seen previously)

First thing the next morning we set off, back through the docks, ditches and locks. At the top on the canal proper, I barrelled ahead as I needed to use the services at Litherland, the other 2 boats followed and said they would wait for me at the swing bridge there.

I got to Litherland, used the services and waited. And waited. No boats. Where were they? Turns out they had gone and left me. They had cruised right past my boat and through the swing bridge whilst I was busy emptying the cassette. The bastards.

That left me with a bit (ha! a bit?) of a stressful problem. I had to get through a particularly tricky swing bridge a couple of hours sail away. It was a timed bridge that was closed to boats between 2pm and 6pm, too busy with cars at rush hour to open the bridge for a lowly boater, you see. If I didn't get through before the bridge automatically locked, I would have to wait 4 hours until I could gain passage, leaving me with only an hour's sailing time in the fading autumnal light. Shit, this was bad. If I didn't get through in time I would have to moor up in bandit country or sail a long way in the dark, through swing bridges and on my own to get to safe mooring. I had wasted precious time waiting for the boat bastards and now I was pushing it to get there.

It was a bloody stressful sail, but I got to the timed bridge, threw the boat against the towpath, ran to the control panel, shoved my key in to begin closing the road and opening the bridge and…nothing happened. The fucking bridge had automatically locked itself 3 minutes previously.

Oh my god. I was stuck. In bandit country, next to a housing estate full of bedrooms with air rifles in them. There was nothing I could do but sit it out. And post on Facebook.

Four hours later I got through the bridge. An hour after that I had no choice but to moor up. I was bricking it, I have to admit. As I was bashing my last mooring pin in, I became aware of a cyclist approaching me and slowing down , here we go, I thought. Trouble, right from the off.

Turns out that cyclist was actually Paul. My boat buddy. He had seen my 'stranded' posting on Facebook whilst he was sailing back from his travels further afield, had turned up the boat revs, got to his home mooring, dragged his bike out and biked the 10 miles to come find me and night cruise me to a safe mooring.

How about that? Triumph over adversity and it was all down to a fortuitous meeting on the cut only months earlier.

Canal life is remarkable. It's like a boiled down version of general life. If you live in a house in a cul de sac, generally you live with the same, like-minded people, who drive similar cars and whose children go to the local school. Nothing at all wrong with that. Live on the cut, however and you can travel down a 1 mile stretch of canal and meet an entire gamut of human nature.

That was never more so than that day. The boat bastards had really, badly let me down. Now Paul was here helping me into another adventure which was night cruising! And it was great fun! Great to have the craic with Paul and his help with the swing bridges and cider topping up. It got even more entertaining when my boat head lamp blew and I had to shimmy down the gunwales with the emergency spot light to navigate by. Then even more entertaining again when that went flat.

Paul eventually moored me up in a safe place, after a 4 hour night cruise, then headed off on his bike along the towpath, back to his own boat in the dead of night. And here's me thinking the only hero I was to meet that day was Sid.

CHAPTER 34

Early Life

It was now time to find the 'dream house'. The house I had promised myself almost 20 years previously, when I was incarcerated in the convent, growing my secret baby.

Except it wasn't that easy, 'course it wasn't. In my mind's eye my dream house had a high spec. My kind of high spec that no house could ever give me without me ripping it out entirely and starting again, and I wanted a house with character, not some soulless new build shell.

Writing this now it's suddenly occurred to me that this is exactly what I did with my little boat too. I just didn't realise it. God I'm slow to catch on sometimes! I bought a boat full of character and fully stripped it out and rebuilt to my own, specific high spec!

Anyway, where was I?

Trying to find a house, which didn't happen, a barn came onto the market instead which seemed to fit our (my) requirements. At least it was an interesting shell to convert into a family home, although small, I was sure I could squeeze all my high spec in.

I set to work scaling, measuring and designing the space whilst the purchase went through, all whilst running around the country on painting commissions.

On the day the deposit was due, I got stuck in a traffic jam.

That enforced time to do nothing but wait, opened up the space in my brain I didn't realise I needed, to simply think.

To think about the choice about buying the barn, to think about the shoe-horn designed space and would it actually work? Was it viable?

No, I had to admit to myself, it wouldn't work and no, it wasn't viable.

I got home hours later and gave the news to the husband, who took it remarkably well. He'd done the same to me a few year's previously before we bought the bank to convert. He bailed on converting his parent's old adjacent barn into a home for us. Barn's were clearly not in our destiny. We pulled out.

The day after we pulled out of the sale, was the day I found the most wrecked old ugly farmhouse strangled by nettles and brambles with trees growing out of gutters and walls.

The estate agent said it was a scrapper, only worth the price of the land it stood on. The owners, however, wanted big money for it as they still lived there and couldn't afford to move out and divorce without the cash. They also wouldn't sell to anyone that wanted to flatten it. Pretty high and unrealistic expectations. Until we came along, that is. We offered them their full asking price. The survey came back reporting it was not worth it. The mortgage company refused to lend us the amount we asked for. This purchase did not bode well. Unnerved yet undeterred we went to a private loan company to make up the short fall. Rash, on a structurally unsound wreck of a building on scrubby sloping land, up a track that vehicles struggled to navigate.

We eventually, after months of negotiation, took possession and hacked our way through the detritus to get to the door that led into our new home. That day I started with a slight twitch in my right eye, which was hardly surprising.

When we finally gained entry by shouldering the door, we could hear the sound of running water that we assumed was a washing machine emptying. It was actually the main water supply freely pouring into the building through a gnawed hole in the pipe, courtesy of one of the several rats that were skittering wildly about.

The previous owners had moved out that day and they had been living like this! It completely beggared belief.

We then began to strip out the farmhouse in earnest. It was very obvious we had dramatically underestimated the magnitude of the erm, restoration.

Before we knew it, we had got ourselves a barn like structure, with riddled walls and floors ripped out.

The most expensive house we and everyone else we knew had ever bought, and now it wasn't even a bloody house!

It's far too close to my boat story for comfort, this is.

Honestly Ok – Dido

If it Makes You Happy – Sheryl Crow

All I Really Want – Alanis Morrissette

CHAPTER 35

A REPRIEVE

She Cries Your Name – Beth Orton

Teardrop – Newton Faulkner

The Sea – Morcheeba

After the drama of Liverpool, I finally admitted to myself it was time to tuck my little boat up for the winter. I cruised back down the hefty Rufford Arm locks and into a marina. I made that sound easy, didn't I?

I'm not even going to bore you with how traumatic it was getting the boat through the narrow mouth of the marina, finding the correct jetty and tightly reversing in between another boat and the wobbly jetty.

I managed it though, I had to leave the boat. I had to concentrate on Jelly.

There was something definitely wrong with Jelly.

It looked like she was slightly dragging her foot. It was weird. The skin on her hands, that she so relied on with creating her ceramic sculptures, had started to crack, burn and peel. Her well-meaning doctor was at an absolute loss, but did suspect an auto immune problem.

Getting an appointment with a rheumatologist consultant however was going to take way too long on the NHS. It was decided that she should try and go private, but where to begin when she had no clue what was actually wrong with her. At least this was something I could help with, I'd been feeling utterly helpless up to this point.

It took a while, but I eventually found a consultant rheumatologist specialising in autoimmune diseases to see her.

However, the day before her appointment, another appointment came through for her. This was with a top rheumatologist consultant through the NHS. A very welcome stroke of luck at last, as knowing what we know now, every penny that she had, was going to be potentially needed for what lay ahead.

Meanwhile November was upon us, a month before Christmas and the weather became unexpectedly beautiful. One of those sparkly winter sunshiny days that you absolutely have to grasp.

Which we did. With both hands. Jel, her partner Peter, and our friends jumped on the boat and went on an outing. It took us 3 hours cruising in the sunshine to get to the local pub, a journey you can do by car in 15 minutes.

It was a welcome distraction of cider drinking and belly laughs, exactly what we all needed.

Who knew the boat was going to soothe not only my soul, but had such a profound and cathartic effect on my friends as well?

The next 2 weeks were a blur of tests and trials for Jelly. Steroids were administered, then increased, then increased further as her body began to fight this bewildering and unknown disease.

On December 8th she was called in for a meeting with several consultants and for a series of tests. One particularly horrendous test involved long needles and electrocution to see how the nerves reacted. It was incredibly traumatic. They did however reach a diagnosis.

On December 8th Jelly was diagnosed with Motor Neurone Disease.

And our world stopped. It was as if we were caught in suspended animation. The shock of the MND diagnosis was just too much to bear, we simply couldn't compute the information.

Then quickly, before we had time to catch our breaths, everything speeded up.

Cocktails of drugs were administered, then altered, as the disease took unexpected turns. The consultants were fire fighting, they couldn't get to grips with all the unusual problems Jel was presenting with. Something just didn't add up.

It was time for us to do some homework and look into her diagnosis a little more closely.

Specifically, could she have been misdiagnosed?

After a lot of research from all of us, I got in touch with the original private consultant I found and discussed the problem with him.

There was a small possibility that she had indeed been misdiagnosed. He explained there was a rare neurological disease that presents similar to MND but had the added complication of a dermatological aspect to it also, which seemed a better fit to Jel's illness as the skin on the base of her feet had almost been eaten away at this point making it agony to walk on.

This little known disease was called Dermatomyositis.

Essentially, this little known disease was a rare neurological disease that you could die with, not from. The thought that she did not have MND, the neurological disease that was 100% terminal, literally felt like a reprieve from the jaws of death.

Further on in the new year after more tests, consultations, hospital stays and more fire fighting of the unusual presentations of the disease, Jelly was eventually and mercifully diagnosed with the much less fatal Dermatomyositis.

A collective huge sigh of relief was made by us all. This was something we could work with.

Frustratingly though, they wouldn't discount the original diagnosis.

So that's Jelly theoretically with 2 rare neurological autoimmune diseases.

I've just googled the chances of this occurring. It's 1 in 14 million.

And that's just bullshit. We knew we had a reprieve with the new diagnosis. Now to go forward and get it managed, as she was getting more poorly by the week. She had now developed a catch in her breath which was unnerving all round.

The next few months were a slog of PET scans, MRI scans, in fact scans that no one had ever even heard of. The PET scan was quite unsettling as Jel had to have radioactive fluid injected into her to enable them to try and detect exactly what her body was suffering from. She was told not to use any toilets other than her own for 24hrs afterward as she would be polluting the sewers with radiation. That's a bloody scary thought she even was allowed it in her system.

Whilst I was waiting in the hospital for her to come out of this scan, I did some research into the disease we hoped she had, as at this stage we were all desperately grasping at any positive we could. I read that there was a 90% survival rate in the first 5 years of contracting DM and an 80% survival rate in the first 10 years.

I also read that 5% of patients die within the first year due to lung complications. There was no doubt about it, Jelly was struggling slightly to breathe. I kept that fact close to my chest and firmly away from her though, obviously.

CHAPTER 36

BOAT BELLEND

Warm Shadow – Fink

Sitting, Waiting Wishing – Jack Johnson

No Bravery – James Blunt

March arrived before I knew it, what with all the hospital stays and visits with Jel.

Also March was the month I had been dreading for a big reason. Kitty was leaving for indefinite travelling in March. My little side kick, always there, always beeping, was leaving for her own adventures with Australia as her final and hopeful permanent destination. I fought hard with my head and my heart, not allowing either to go into a tailspin with her departure.

Instead, I focussed on my saviour, that little 30' narrowboat.

It was now time to dig my little boat out again. I had spent a good few weeks retouching the paintwork from all the bashes and scrapes she had received over that first season of learning to boat. The windows were still leaking even though I'd had them out trying to fix them less than a year ago. It was like owning an expensive colander when a heavy downpour hit, the boat the windows leaked like they were crying (I know I was at least, for so many reasons, in fact I just couldn't stop crying) However, I realised there were some things you just had to get over. I was realising this a lot and quickly with all the problems that were occurring with Jel.

I had to pull myself together as this was now the time to get ready for filming! The pilot film we made 6 months previously had been approved by Channel 4 and a series of 20 episodes were commissioned. The series was to be called 'Narrow Escapes' and I had been invited to take part.

The TV production company were excited about filming my new season's adventures.

This year I had a bucket list of boat travels I really wanted to do. In fact it was a promise I had made to myself in the very early, anxious and panicked days of the Dawn Piper's restoration. This bucket list is what kept me positive and focused and now was going to become a reality. Except now they wanted to film me doing it! The nervy poos came back with a vengeance as my stress levels rose to Defcon 1.

The reason for my stress was that I really wasn't convinced I could look anything better than a profound boat bellend on (or off, to be honest) camera.

Therefore I decided I had to practice! I took my son Teddy as moral support (read that as hostage) on the new season's practice maiden voyage.

I booted the old girl up from the jetty in the marina where she had bobbed patiently around for winter, put her in reverse and she immediately shoved forwards slamming into the front of the jetty.

Oh shit, this boded badly. I couldn't even remember which gear was reverse, and there were only two of them to choose from!

I sheepishly sneaked out of the marina that day and turned right towards the first lock. I had to relearn everything I had forgotten and quickly. First up was single handing through a lock. The production company wanted to film my single handed boat life. At this point, it was still quite unusual (read that as downright foolhardy) for a female to buy a narrowboat, restore and refit it then learn how to move it single handedly from absolute beginner status.

I got it all wrong, of course I did. It did not help that filming was beginning in a matter of days. However, Ted was great. He patiently went though it all with me and calmed my tattered nerves. Which was just as well as the next hurdle was opening the heavy manual swing bridge.

As I've explained earlier, manual swing bridges are a pain in the arse, as my little boat struggles to moor up in the weeds offside in order for me to open the bridge.

I had hatched a cunning manoeuvre to overcome this. I just needed to check how cunning it was, as the 'rope trick' I had in mind seemed so simple, I couldn't imagine anyone hadn't thought of it before.

It only went and bloody worked though!

Essentially, I moored up towpath side, crossed the bridge and unlocked it, looped a long piece of rope around the nearest stanchion of the bridge, walked back over the bridge and used the rope to pull the bridge open. Bloody boat genius right there!

Now feeling less like a boat bellend, I set off again, heading for the next lock. Except I didn't get there. The damn boat was overheating again and I knew it would be prudent to turn her around and head back to the safety of the marina.

The Rufford Arm of the Leeds-Liverpool canal, known unaffectionately as the Weeds-Liverpool canal, is notorious for being choked in Pennywort weed, making it difficult to moor up, jump off and flick the boat around using my ropes. This was a technique I had been practising on narrow canals for just this reason. If I had to turn the boat around, I didn't have to travel an hour upstream to the nearest winding hole. That's one of the joys of having a baby narrowboat, I suppose.

With my newly acquired and self rewarded boat genius status, I decided to moor up under a big railway bridge, get my butter knife out, undo the jubilee clip and blow down the water inlet pipe to try and free the blockage that was causing the boat to overheat, yet again.

That achieved, it was time to flick the boat around in order to retrace our steps.

I had Ted videoing this on my phone as I wanted to show my skills off on TikTok to prove how accomplished I was.

All was going well until the optimum moment where the boat straddling the canal is supposed to gently turn to come back on herself. Except she didn't. I got her fully stuck like a cork in a bottle, right across the narrower-than-gauged width of the canal. Fuuuccckkkk.

Teddy's clip of me doing this did make it on to TikTok, however. 650K people watched it. 650K people watching me make a massive boat bellend out of myself.

The camera never lies, it seems.

CHAPTER 37

FILMING (OH GOD)

Shut Your Eyes – Snow Patrol

Mexican Standoff – Elbow

Busted – The Black Keys

The only stipulation I gave to Heidi, the series producer of the production company was that I could not safely single hand up through the 7 locks, and on to the end of the day's filming if it was raining and / or windy. Too slippy in the wet and too hard to rope and keep in control if windy.

Filming was set for 23rd of March, a day of questionable weather, but positivity from most, including Sean the cameraman and James the runner. Not me though, I was shitting it.

The rain held off until Sean began filming. Then it gained momentum and began chucking it down. At this point, we were in it to win it, so just had to push on through.

It took 8 hours of hard graft to get up the locks and through the 4 swing bridges. This was due to the torrential rain and high winds. At one point I struggled with the boat so much it looked like she was trying to turn herself around and head back to the moorings. I broke down 3 times, one of those times was actually me. The boat overheated so profoundly that I had to get my new fix-it tool, a bike pump, out to attach it to the inlet pipe and blow the blockage free. My breakdown happened internally when Sean, now filming with a drone, asked me to keep pumping away on my new fix-it tool for a good 20 minutes whilst he got the shots.

I was bollocksed but still had 4 more locks and 3 swing bridges to do before I could collapse. Which I did profoundly after 2 pints in the Windmill on arrival in Parbold.

Before that, however, I was filmed asking a passer-by for help with an automatic swing bridge which he refused to do, making me look like a desperate woman trying to pull a bloke into marriage. He ran off, and the tv crew were delighted. Humiliation makes good television, apparently. That's me going down well on C4 then ffs.

Then we came across the actual boat I bought when I was pissed in the bath before I purchased the Dawn Piper. Now I looked like an alcoholic and desperate woman crash-cruising a narrowboat in the wind and rain. Great, just great.

And this was only day 1 of filming.

At least Jel was living this drama vicariously through me. It was an entertaining distraction for her as she was constantly in and out of hospital being a guinea pig for all sorts of trial drugs and infusions that the consultants were desperately trying to stabilise her with.

I continued with my new season's adventures, all the while staying in touch with Jelly.

The next scheduled filming was in Manchester, which took a few day's sailing to get there.

Along the way, I had arranged to see my boat buddy Paul in Wigan, for a couple of pints. We were going to meet up further down the line and cruise together, so this was just a catch up. Except I got distracted by an exotically pretty man sitting alone at a table. Paul's eyes rolled. He'd seen this behaviour from me towards my potential hostages, I mean boyfriends, before.

Just a quick note for you: if I ever ask you to help me through some locks that I can't manage, RUN. That would be best practise, I promise you.

This poor bugger hadn't got the memo, however, and did agree to help me up the locks the following day.

Jel called him Boat Ornament. Which I know is somewhat satirical, but she was ill and in my eyes, could get away with anything. So the nickname stuck.

I had snagged a new plaything, erm, boyfriend for the new season!

Sailing into Castlefield Basin just like before, was superb. Jules joined me and out on the town we went. As ever with Jules, we got a bit carried away. Getting back fully steaming to the boat I decided to move her to a more quiet mooring away from all the Canadian geese that thronged on the towpath to fight and shag noisily all night, which I duly did.

Waking up the next morning confused the bejesus out of me as I found myself moored in an entirely different position with no knowledge of having moved the boat the previous evening. Not a proud moment, that one and one I definitely blame Jules for. "Course I do.

Before this and whilst I was buggering about getting to Manchester, the production company were negotiating filming costs and terms with the National Trust. I had mentioned to them about the beguiling encounter Jel and I had after mooring up at Dunham Massey, with the stag the year previously and they wanted to try and capture a similar encounter on film.

Full disclosure: I wasn't moored up there when we filmed the scenes at the deer park there. We drove to the location. We really wanted a beautiful sunset and with all the rain we had, the weather wasn't guaranteed, so we faked it a bit.

But it was so worth it! White stags moved nonchalantly around us, herds of deer grazed in the setting sun whilst frisky young bucks gambolled and leapt in front of us. It was utterly bewitching and made great tele.

Which was a huge relief all round. The production company that initially pitched the concept of following people living and working on narrowboats to Channel 4, was a small indie company of 9 core people. None of these people had ever been near a narrowboat, never mind on one. So they were on a massive learning curve of logistics and trust.

It was an absolute logistical nightmare for them to get a car, crew and equipment to the boats and locations to be filmed. Boaters are renowned for not keeping to a schedule, plan or even direction, it was like herding cats for the team.

Throw in bad weather, muddy towpaths, cramped conditions, and the boater's assurances of their story's being tele worthy, it's a wonder they got any valuable footage at all. Hence choosing a lovely evening for filming the deer.

The fact that all that footage was lost, never to be recovered was a slight downer, if you could call it that. In fact they didn't call it that , they called it a downright fucking disaster and something that had to be re-shot weeks later when we all had space in our calendars.

Guess what? The evening we re-shot the deer scene, was the evening there were barely any deer there, there were, however, lots of Japanese tourists getting into shot. We ended up sinking in a bog trying to lose the tourists, the deer spooked and ran off…you get the idea. The new footage was shit.

I found out very early on that the mantra of 'let the editors deal with it' was very often used.

CHAPTER 38

EARLY YEARS

It took us 10 weeks of hard graft, sinusitis, bronchitis and nervous collapse to get our expensive ripped out shit hole of a house cleanish and liveable ish. We moved into the first floor, set up kitchen on the landing, and lived and slept in the bedrooms. We put a gate on the stairs to keep baby Ted from falling and our nasty cocker spaniel (a poor substitute for my adored bad dog Joe Bell) from eating baby Ted. My nesting, however, had to be temporarily put on hold.

Now was the time to concentrate on the interior design and bespoke furniture shop we had in a nearby town. Money was fast becoming an issue.

Well, it was fast becoming an issue with me. I never, and to this day ever, knew or found out how much money my husband made. Apart from moaning how much tax he had to pay, he kept all his finances entirely separate from mine. I had to bring my own money in. Which was okay, although it did put a stress on things now having an 18 month old. At least the rental income from the converted bank helped pay some of the domestic bills. Which was a blessed relief as before I knew it, I found myself pregnant again. A small miracle, as all the hassle with Ted's conception led me to believe another pregnancy would be another trauma.

Which it turned out to be anyway. Placenta Praevia made sure of that. Because of the placenta covering my cervix, it meant my pregnancy was under constant threat and I couldn't work, leaving me alarmingly short of funds. Therefore, to appease my nesting urges, I took up a cheap form of completing the finishing touches on the now complete-enough farmhouse, which was sewing.

I made covers for the sofas, curtains, I embroidered blankets, cushions and curtains for the new baby's room, all whilst having the joy of time playing with baby Ted.

This enforced time out made me realise even more is that money comes and money goes in life. What truly mattered was my children. This is what I had dreamed of, I just got a little distracted by building a home for them for 6 months.

It was also the excuse I needed for closing the shop we had. I could live off Sir Peter's commissions when they occasionally came in.

That reminds me of one commission I had done recently for him. I was applying a paint effect to the ceiling in his dining room, up scaffolding. Ted was 10 months old and I had weaned him off breastfeeding and onto formula especially so I could take the commission on. I had to, as I said, I had to bring my own money in.

As soon as the commission began, Ted contracted gastroenteritis, and the doctor advised a return to breastfeeding for him. Ted had to be imported to the site every 4 hours for days by my mother so that I could take my respiration gear off, climb down from the scaffolding and feed my baby. Fucking nuts and something that a lack of my husband's funding caused me to have to do.

I think you can see where this is heading…anyway, that's a few years off yet.

Back to the joy of babies! My beautiful Kitty was born on 23rd October by C-Section.

She was whisked off to be fed and tested because of the gestational diabetes I had been suffering from. Thank god I'd had a girl and I never had to be pregnant again. My body just could not take another beating.

She beeped at me from the day she was born, could never be apart from me. I couldn't even have a wee without her beeping. So I took her everywhere with me, even the loo!

There began the second deep bond I was to cherish and never part with. My soul gave a small sigh of relief. I now had my longed for, yearned for children in the forever family home that I promised to myself 20 years previously.

More Than Words – Extreme

Nothing Compares 2 U – Sinead O'Connor

Beautiful Day – U2

CHAPTER 39

ENEMY TERRITORY

This Love Is Over – Ray LaMontagne and The Pariah Dogs

Enjoy The Ride – Morcheeba

Half The World Away – Oasis

Next up on my bucket list and next up for filming was the Anderton Boat Lift. I hadn't done it the previous year as it had been closed for restoration. I was booked on as one of the first to use it since its reopening. Very Exciting! Except very nerve racking, but not for the reasons you would imagine.

My ex, the boat boyfriend (Jel called him 'that fat bastard boat bully', she was pretty astute to be fair) was now working at the boat lift as skipper of the trip boat that ferried throngs of excited canal lovers up and down the lift.

He was definitely going to be there. The reason for my trepidation was that when I had bumped into him in a supermarket after we'd split, he was absolutely vile to me, which only confirmed Jelly's name for him. Now I too was a boater, he would definitely think I was trying to out trump him.

I could feel my blood pressure rising as I moored up the day before we were due to film. And sure enough, as I moored up in a nervy fumble, he cruised his boat past me, towing another stricken boat behind him. Like the hero in a western, riding into town and saving the day. Bollocks. All I was doing was tying up badly, arse in the air and hair everywhere. The thought of getting through the next day's filming looking like a total bellend became an even bigger reality. I was surely doomed.

The morning arrived, the crew turned up promptly and the sun mercifully shone.

So far so good. Then the producer, said we needed to film the sequence in reverse order, something to do with timings, I believe. Shit, I'd have to pretend I'd already come down the lift when I hadn't even booted the engine up. To make matters worse, the trip boat was there with Him at the helm, there were hundreds of visitors mulling around, then rubber necking and craning to see what all the fuss was about with a camera crew filming and me faking having been on the trip of a lifetime going down this historic boat lift (oh god)

To be honest, I ended up seeing the funny side of it. I couldn't wait to tell Jel I was being filmed stood in front of the huge glass topped trip boat, with all the passengers watching, all facing towards me and the film crew, bar one person, who was resolutely facing the opposite way, as if he would turn to stone by catching a glimpse of me. I know this as I was surreptitiously watching him. In fact I quite impressed myself with my multitasking skills that day: stalking whilst talking whilst walking whilst being filmed. Catchy phrase for a future life, that one.

I recently came up with another catchy phrase regarding swinging and dogging – but I might save you from that one. For now.

Anyway, where was I?

To add to my mirth, all the boat lift big-wigs came out for a PR handshake with me and I couldn't help but mention to them that their skipper was my ex as they took photographs for their internal newsletter and as they burned their eyes into the back of his head. Oh the joy of it.

They call the Anderton Boat Lift one of the 7 wonders of the canal network. It is an iconic and incredible feat of Victorian engineering. Opened in 1875, this two caisson lift carried tons of salt on up to 30 boats a day, up onto the Trent and Mersey canal. This enabled a far more efficient route to reach the factories and market towns of the midlands and beyond.

I felt extremely privileged to be going down it and nervously excited about it taking me onto the River Weaver.

It was a bit bamboozling filming that day as there was so much going on. We did several takes of me walking around the grounds, talking about my 'trip' down the lift. Going into the Visitor Centre, buying a 'keepsake' mug to be used for filming at the end of the day, all the while word was spreading that there was a film crew, with every one (yes, bar Him) watching.

Then it was time to come down the lift on the Dawn Piper. To say I was mildly shitting it would be an understatement. I had to manoeuvre the boat through a sharp left turn and position her at the correct caisson. As you might remember,

I'm rubbish with my left and right. The only difference between an open caisson and a shut one was what looked like a narrow metal ridge spanning the width of the closed caisson, something easy to miss if I chose the wrong one. Except submerged beneath the water, that metal ridge was actually a guillotine gate and if I accidentally rammed the boat into that it would see the newly multi-million-pound restored and opened boat lift shut down again. Which would be bad. Very bad.

I managed to get myself into the correct tank, tie up and talk through what was happening as I descended, to the camera. I did seem pretty batshit to be honest, as clearly I had no idea what was going on, but thankfully with the wonders of technology, the crew were happy with the footage.

Then before I knew it, my little boat was out onto the mighty River Weaver, swimming like a little minnow in a vast calm sea. I felt complete denial of breaking down the best place to be, because if I thought about the logistics of it, I would be well and truly knackered. No where to moor, too deep to mud anchor (not that I knew how to, anyway). I have to say though, nerves aside it was truly serene being on such a vast body of water, it felt like I was gliding along the deep, clear river.

Filming over, I breathed a sigh of relief. Now I could relax. The next filming was scheduled in a month's time, at the end of May. My final bucket list destination, the indefatigable Pontcysyllte Aqueduct, a UNESCO World Heritage site and another of the 7 wonders of the canal system. But before that, a quick chill bobbing around on the beguiling river before I moored her up to jump off and check on Jelly.

CHAPTER 40

A VERY NEAR MISS

Teardrop – Newton Faulkner

Pressure Drop – Toots and the Maytals

When the Levee Breaks – Led Zeppelin

I had to get back home to flip the house as well as to see Jelly. There was no Kitty at home, she was still travelling and my boys were always busy with their own lives, which was just as well. Between the Airbnb of my farmhouse, filming schedules and Jelly's illness, I was hard pushed to fit the new boyfriend in, as it were.

My mum's suggestion of Airbnbing the house had certainly paid off. I was busier than ever flipping it for new guests. The revenue from it enabled my boat life and paid the mortgage, so that part of my life was going well.

The part that saw my best friend in all the world getting more poorly in hospital was alarming bad though, to say the very least.

Jel was now on oxygen full time. Her neck had swollen up so profoundly that it was the width of her head. They suspected a perforated oesophagus.

The day she had the scan to confirm or deny this, saw me sitting by her bedside with her, awaiting the results. I'd hidden some fancy cakes under the bed, in the hope she did not have to rushed off and operated on if indeed it was confirmed. Man alive she was so brave. She kept repeating she had to be for her 14 year old son. Mercifully, the scan came back negative, our relief was again palpable as we feasted on the hidden cakes, handing them out to everyone on the ward as a small celebration and win from the cruel disease she was fighting so hard.

With Jel's reprieve and yet another flip of the house, I returned to the boat, this time with my boat ornament boyfriend. I was determined to sail the entire navigable length of the River Weaver. I wanted to moor rurally, light bonfires and swim in the river. I also wanted to practice getting on and off the boat by myself. It had been a thing for me to ensure I could get back on my boat safely and successfully, in case of catastrophe. It's much more difficult than you can imagine trying to get on a boat from water. Your legs automatically swing under the hull of the boat making it near impossible to pull yourself out and onto the gunwhales.

I eventually reached the perfect mooring to try testing the technique that I had in my tiny mind of alighting back on the boat from the river.

I chose a quiet and still early morning with no one else around to gently shimmy into the water from the boat and have a bit of a swim around. All good so far, if somewhat Baltic. Now was the moment of truth. Getting back on board. I swam to the back of the boat, put one foot on the skeg (the shelf that supports the rudder and protects the propeller) and began to try and lever myself up with the tiller.

It was at the point when the tiller swung out leaving me dangling at 45 degrees out from the back end of the boat, I heard a strange swishing noise. It certainly wasn't a boat, thank god, but the noise was a mystery nonetheless.

Just as I managed to haul myself up on the back fender whist swinging wilding from side to side holding the tiller as a bad idea for support, an all man rowing team swooshed by, right at the point I had straddled one leg over the side rail before landing in a wet humph on the back deck.

All I can say is I only wish to god I hadn't been naked doing it. Those poor men might never recover.

I loved the Weaver. I did indeed moor rurally, light bonfires and traverse the whole navigable river. It was an entirely different experience than being on the canal. Once I stopped fretting about breaking down, I had an overwhelming sense of freedom sailing along on that vast meandering river. With no towpaths, it felt as if I were an explorer breaking into new territory, mooring on deep river banks, collecting firewood to burn in the fire pit whist watching fish jumping to catch flies as the sun began to set. I found it truly beguiling.

There is of course another side to the River Weaver, that still connects to the Manchester ship canal, which at the turn of the 19th century afforded easy passage of salt and other goods to the nearby port of Liverpool. This allowed enormous canal tugs to tow strings of laden barges from the salt mines of Cheshire onto the further reaches of the country.

A relic of this era and still in use today is the SS Daniel Adamson, or the Danny as the boat is more affectionately known. Built in 1903, she is a unique combination of Edwardian tugboat and Art Deco passenger ferry. At 110 feet long and 25 feet wide, you could fit about 64 Dawn Pipers in her. She's bloody massive.

I still shudder to this day at what happened…

On the day in question I was just bimbling along on my boat, when I saw the Danny ahead of me, loading passengers. As we were heading in the same direction I thought it would be quite cool to follow her. Remember, I'm not cool at anything, you should see me dancing to prove that.

Now the locks and swing bridges on the Weaver are something to behold. They too are massive. These are operated by lock keepers. As we approached the lock and the Danny successfully tied up within it, I realised there was still room for me, so I blagged my way in to sharing the lock with the Danny, to some consternation about safety because if the Danny came loose, she could squash me like a fly using a steamroller to do so, as the lockies explained. I was happy to take the risk though, as in my mind it was a once in a lifetime experience to be up so close and personal with such an enormous and historic vessel

I know you're now thinking 'oh god' but actually it was totally drama free and a very enjoyable experience. So there.

The trouble came later.

As we approached the Anderton Boat Lift and the only place where the Danny could turn around, she slowed down which was expected, so I held back and came to a stop on the left of her. Passing large vessels is the same as passing small ones, you do so on the right.

No problem I thought, I'll just wait till she's turned then get past her.

To double check I was okay with doing this, I gesticulated to Danny's crew, who gesticulated back. I should have also double checked what their gesticulations actually meant, because as I nipped past with the giant concrete mooring landing on my left and the fucking massive steam ship on my right, a man on the dock started waving frantically and shouting at me. Unfortunately, I worked out what he was saying a little too late, which was something that is now indelible in my brain and still ringing in my ears. He was shouting 'get back, get back, she's docking, you're going to be crushed'.

Fuck my days, he was right. The gap between the mooring and the Danny was closing in at the stern and I was well over half way through passing her. I couldn't turn back, I had to power on. I ramped up the revs to full chat and got through the gap with literally inches to spare. I actually have a photo to prove it. That photo came from one of the 110 souls on board that day that were all watching me nearly kill myself but worse still, it was the most uncool thing anyone has ever managed to achieve in the long, long history of the Daniel Adamson.

You honestly couldn't imagine my horror. I moored up round the corner, out of humiliating sight and booked myself on the boat lift to go up onto the canal for the very next day. It was time to leave the river and a far cry from when I smugly came onto the Weaver 10 days before with all the hand shakes and camera crew and fascinated tourists.

CHAPTER 41

EARLY YEARS

Now with our 2 babies growing like weeds, we all got into the swing of family life. Well, kind of. Husband was always busy, I still managed to encourage him to help do the house up though, slowly but surely. We were now living on 2 floors which made life a bit easier. It also meant I could trap that bloody mean dog of ours in the utility room. He still bit me every day, but at least the threat of the children being bitten was minimalised. Husband still wasn't having any of the dog's bad behaviour though as the little bastard was always good around him. That was just one small niggle in a panful of niggles that was on a slow simmer.

He was a good dad though. He played with the kids every night when he got home and only went out to meetings or the gym after they were in bed. Although slow, the work he was doing on the house also was beautiful. Being a cabinet maker and with both of us as furniture designers, the interior fit out was exceptional.

Ted's bedroom for instance, was fitted out in pippy oak with an elevated bunk bed. I painted a jungle mural over his bedroom walls and I used plastic geckos' I found in a toy shop as handles on his cupboards. It was this level of detail we were good at together.

Unfortunately the niggles were still there though, even if we both did our best to stave them off, he was definitely as pissed of with me as I was with him and with good cause to be fair.

As an example of this, one time I kept hearing a strange crackling noise in the house near the eaves. When I mentioned it on several occasions to my spouse, he said it was birds nesting. But it wasn't nesting season.

The fact that it was not birds nesting came to light on a particular day whilst I was doing my bit too with the house. It was when Ted was at primary school and Kitty was having her nap. I was up on the makeshift scaffolding painting the exterior of the house with the baby monitor strapped to me, when I poked my paintbrush into a spongy crackling something, near the eaves of the house. This set off an alarming chain of events as the hornets in the nest that had been munching their way through the eaves and then onto our bedroom ceiling, surged backwards from my paintbrush and the whole nest collapsed through the ceiling, filling the bedroom with angry, scary hornets.

All I can say is thank god the bedroom door was shut. I virtually threw myself off the scaffolding, charged up to Kit's room and hoofed an alarmed toddler out of bed and down the stairs to relative safety.

Something was going to have to give. It felt like I was back in the years before children again, when husband used to walk around the house wearing ear defenders when I was the only other person there! Funny, not funny that one.

I realise now that around this time I subliminally set off my own chain of events. Beginning with rehoming that bastard dog.

Kitty Jay – Seth Lakeman

I'm No Angel – Dido

What Do You Want From Me – Pink Floyd

CHAPTER 42

SPRINGING A LEAK

Picky Bugger – Elbow

Coal – Dylan Gossett

Longing to Belong – Eddie Vedder

With the near catastrophe of the Weaver firmly behind me it was time to begin my adventure up the Llangollen canal. I'd heard so much about this bewitching canal, about it's beauty, the stunning scenery and incredible feats of engineering, I couldn't wait to get started.

However, I needed to go to Nantwich first, pick up supplies, fill up with water which I seemed to be using rather a lot of and meet up with my boat buddy Paul who was going to come up the Llangollen at the same time. We tended to meet up occasionally in this way, never travelling far together but often catching up with one another along the way.

Hang on. I was using more water than normal…ohforchristsake, please say I hadn't done it again. I'd done this once before, crash moored the boat and ripped the water tank overflow off the outside of the bow. There's a quick way to check this which is peeling back the Lino and lifting the floorboards in the galley.

Which I realised I had to now do again and oh holy Jesus, the bottom of the boat was yet again, full of water.

The production company had left me a GoPro camera for use in such situations as this makes good tele you see? So I filmed myself bailing the water out and text the producer what had happened. The camera crew arrived the very next day, because it does indeed make good tele.

They filmed me speaking to Big John, my engineer on the phone, asking for his help. It was actually his wife, Julie who had been on the other end, I was making the whole conversation up. I was beginning to realise that these small details did sometimes have to be faked for continuity and narrative purposes but it didn't take away from the truth of the story. It just meant I had to up my game to make it more believable. John got to do his filming debut and gave me the diagnosis on camera. It transpired I hadn't scuttled my own boat by crashing her, a seal had popped off the overflow causing me to overfill the tank and inadvertently try to sink my boat from the inside out.

And they caught all that on camera too. Me. Being a boat bellend. Again.

I kept in touch with Jelly constantly during this time, trying to distract her with my stupid stories whilst she was poked and prodded, filled with a toxic array of meds and shoved through all manner of scans.

Then she phoned me. This was a biggy as she was on so much oxygen because of the scarring the disease was doing to her lungs, she didn't have enough breath to speak. She'd had a seizure, she told me. A seizure. The doctors had pumped her so full of drugs that her body was shutting down because of them. But if she didn't have the drugs, her lungs would collapse. Panic was setting in with the doctors, never mind us.

I was helpless. Visits were very limited due to infection risks. They were talking about fully stripping out her immune system and rebooting it, but she had such a high temperature, they daren't try it. It was getting bad. This disease was horribly aggressive and the doctor's fire fighting just wasn't working.

Then the doctors began to talk about a plan B.

I needed to keep busy, not spiral out of control, that would have been no good to anyone. Thankfully it was time to begin the journey towards my final adventure of crossing the Pontcysyllte Aqueduct, right near the end of the 42 mile long bewitching Llangollen canal.

My mate Jules jumped on to help me up the locks, however the real reason was that we needed the support of each other, as Jelly battled her dreadful illness. Between Paul following on his boat and Jules helping on mine, we made a great little team up and off we went, up the Golley. First stop Wrenbury and the Dusty Miller pub.

Jules jumped off here, Paul hung back, doing boat jobs and I continued solo

I made great progress up the Golley and dodged as many of the hired narrowboats as I could. It's a thing on the Llangollen canal, hire boaters. Now I like hire boaters, however they are reviled by many, which is entirely unfair in my opinion. All they're doing is trying to have a blissful and serene, quintessentially British canal boating holiday in as much luxury as humanly possible, whilst navigating one of the busiest waterways in the country and it costing them multi thousands of pounds for the privilege. However, more usually they're navigating in the pissing rain and howling wind.

The argument is that hire boaters can't manoeuvre the boats properly. Which is rich, given that I'd say 60% of the live aboard boating community is constantly pissed whilst moving their boats. Probably why I like boating so much then.

They do tend to hire inordinately and unnecessarily long boats though. Great long steel crashing tubes. I met a couple of Americans at the services along the way, hire boats are always at the services filling up with water. They use the boat's resources as if in a hotel on dry land. Anyway, this couple were on a 70' long boat. Massive. He looked happy as a pig in shit, she looked like she was eating the shit the pig was in.

I asked them how come they hired such a long boat? She said a couple of friends were joining them for a weekend of their 2 week hire and her husband didn't like sharing a bathroom. What The Actual Fuck?

The Golley is renowned for being narrow and shallow with lots of tight corners. I'll be honest and say it did come as a source of amusement watching the hire boaters. Usually the women on the front, popping up like mere cats with their walkie talkies, barking to the beer drinking men on the back about an impending boat approaching from 100 metres away. With the skipper in his captain's hat then careening to the right in an avoidance panic and becoming profoundly grounded in the silt doing so.

It actually got to be a thing throwing ropes to the poor sods to pull them off the mud banks they were sat on.

 The Llangollen Canal is also renowned for its outstanding beauty and breathtaking views. Elevated above the Welsh countryside, the canal winds through rolling hills with long reaching views and the meandering River Dee far below.

There are two notable aqueducts along this stretch, the first being Chirk. I had heard about its remarkable feat of engineering, where a railway viaduct is above and the canal aqueduct below, spanning the river 70' beneath. But nothing prepared me for the sheer scale of it. Rounding the corner on my little boat, I was struck not only by its magnitude but by its utter beauty.

Then on through Chirk tunnel which leads you out into a deep cutting in the hillside, shrouded in trees. Two minutes previously I been cruising 70' up with vast views of vales outstretched before me, now I felt as if I'd popped up in another land. This was without doubt an awe inspiring canal.

I pushed on, every corner revealing some other gem until I eventually reached the Poncysyllte Aqueduct.

Man alive, I had seen photos, watched videos and read blogs but never was I expecting this! From rural bliss to people and boats everywhere! It had a kind of carnival atmosphere to it. And I could absolutely see why. The Aqueduct. Oh my god.

This was the pinnacle of my adventures and probably one of the last vestiges of a profound lack of health and safety left in the UK today. Because fuck me, there's only 100mm of iron, no railings, nothing to prevent you losing your balance, tipping off the back of the boat and tumbling the 126 feet into the vast chasm beneath you. Which was easily done because of the narrow channel of water you were traversing, whilst constantly bumping into the sides of the iron tank that was the aqueduct.

So now here I was, 5 days before filming my crossing of this notorious aqueduct, on the precipice of completing my goal. All I had to do was wait.

Not. A. Fucking. Chance.

I got on that aqueduct as fast as I could. Yes, it was shit scary. Yes, it's probably best to do it with a couple of pints of cider in you to blunt the nerves. But it absolutely is one of the most superb canal experiences I could ever have imagined.

Chapter 43

Early Life

We limped on with the marriage. Husband knew I wouldn't split our young family up. Knew I loved the house so much and couldn't afford to live in it without keeping the marriage intact. It became a kind of abandonment. Well, his side was. My side was nearer to ticking time bomb. I just needed to get the kids as grown up as possible, in the best family unit I could manage.

I towed caravans to family destinations, with husband arriving days later after camp was established and leaving before it was time to pack up and come home.

I took the kids to Spanish apartments, hiring cars and navigating in the dark to get to our holiday home, with husband flying in for me to pick him up in said hire car, then duly return him to the airport so he could fly back before us.

It was shit.

We continued in this vain until a violent episode caused me to snap. It was bound to happen. Tension just reached boiling point and before we all knew it, the marriage ended.

It wasn't that easy, obvs. I'll just not bore you with the tears, recriminations and financial threats. Too many of us have been there, each story different but usually heartbreakingly similar.

I write this today, totally coincidentally 10 years to the day that I uttered the words 'I've had enough' Just those 3 words. And it changed the course of our lives. For better, for worse. For richer or poorer. And my god, it really was for a long time after that.

I'm going to break here from writing. Get a bottle of champagne out of the fridge and toast all the 10 year down the line divorces. Because fuck me, we deserve it x.

Passing Stranger – Scott Matthews

We're Not Right – David Gray

Waiting On An Angel – Ben Harper

CHAPTER 44

THE END OF THE LINE

5 Year's Time – Noah And The Whale

You're Gonna Go Far – Noah Kahan

Without You – Eddie Vedder

Jelly's plan B was as suspected, for the consultants to fully take her immune system out. Reboot the whole thing. I was hoping they would put her in an induced coma, the same as they did with my brother 11 years previously. You'd think it would be traumatic seeing someone you love in a coma, obviously it is, but it's also a relief knowing they can have some peace whilst the doctors worked their magic on them. It certainly worked for my brother, thankfully. However, they couldn't do this with Jelly. It was because of her lungs. Apparently because they were perforated, the respirator would not be effective, rather like pumping air into popped tyres.

I still couldn't see her at this stage, the infection risk was still too high.

So I continued distracting myself with boat life. I couldn't have had a lovelier distraction than crossing the aqueduct and getting to the other side.

To me it felt like I'd come across a whole new canal on the other side.

This canal was really narrow and twisty. Most hire boaters tended to cross the aqueduct, tick the box, turn round and power back.

Hire boaters get a lot of criticism for going too fast. This is because they're mostly on a tight schedule of pick the boat up from the hire company, have 30 minutes rushed tuition on how to move, moor and manage the boat, jump on board with a dozen slabs of Stella, a few captains hats and throw the boat down the canal and back, all in 7 days. Takes me 2 days cruising to get a takeaway from the curry house!

The section of canal that stretches from the Pontcysyllte aqueduct to the Llangollen basin is notorious. This section is home to the Llangollen Narrows. One boat wide sections of canal teetering on the side of hewn out Welsh hillside, where you should take a crew member to walk ahead to ensure there are no approaching boats and the coast is clear.

I wasn't about to do that, I didn't need to go that far up the canal. After pulling yet another hire boat out of the mud, all I wanted to do was moor at a location with a magnificent view, sunbathe, drink and wait for Paul to catch me up.

Which he did, three days before filming and on that same day I got a call to say I could go and visit Jelly.

Did you ever see the part of Forrest Gump where he gets news his mother is ill when he's on his boat? He immediately jumps off and swims ashore to get to her.

That's what I felt like I was doing when I got the green light to see Jel.

I had massive trepidation walking along the corridor to her room that day, worried sick about what I might find. Do you know what though? She looked great. Well, a lot better than my previous visit. The swelling in her neck had gone down, she was sat up in bed sparkly eyed and chatting, albeit through an oxygen mask, but it looked like she was actually turning a corner. It looked like the doctors had finally got her meds correct.

It was just bliss being in the same room as her. I told her of my exploits which always entertained her and listened when she told me what the doctors had been doing to achieve this small win of recovery. It was a huge relief and delight seeing her again.

I returned to my boat the next day a proper happy bunny.

Which was profoundly short lived, it turned out.

The next day, the sun was shining, Paul was busy buggering about with his boat and I decided to go on a little cruise out solo, couldn't resist.

I fired little boat up, set off, and before I'd got too far past Paul's boat she had overheated to alarming proportions. That's pulling bloody hire boats out of the mud for you, I'd obviously sucked a load of shite up and blocked the inlet pipe again.

Fucking boat.

Paul dragged me back to my mooring by my ropes and I set about with my old butter knife trick of removing the inlet pipe and clearing the blockage. Except it didn't work. Nothing did. It looked like this time, I was properly broken down. Shit. Now what to do. I'm in the middle of Welsh Wales, on a rural canal high above civilisation. Big John is on holiday. They're filming me crossing the fucking Aqueduct in 2 fucking days and I'm properly broken down on the wrong fucking side of the damn thing!

Shit.

Then Paul reminded me I had RCR cover. River Canal Rescue, the boating equivalent of the RAC. Turned out it was expired cover, fucks sake, I renewed at great cost over the phone and they returned the favour by sending a mechanic out to fix the problem. We were back in business it seemed.

Is it my age, or are all trades getting younger and younger? A lovely baby faced mechanic turned up. Said he'd never worked on anything like my pump before, dismantled it, confirmed it was knackered and told me he'd send it away to be fixed. But it could take 6 weeks to get it back!!

What?? I thought mechanics could fix stuff?

The growing realisation I was in big trouble was beginning to hit in epic proportions.

The film crew had filmed my adventure in chronological order for the most part. The day after tomorrow would be the last day of filming. For everyone. The crew and the company were straight onto a new project the day after filming my last adventure, the one I'd been talking about right the way through on camera. The journey's end. And I'm stuck completely broken down on the wrong side of the aqueduct. What the fuck could I do now?

I slumped into my deck chair on the towpath, the wind completely knocked out of me. Suddenly it wasn't a sunny halcyon day anymore. Suddenly it felt like I was looking down the barrel of a gun. I was not looking forward to telling Heidi the series producer this one.

Then Paul walked past and muttered the words jokingly 'I could always tow you'

I could always tow you. Fuck me, he could always tow me!! Of course!

I let the relief and cider wash over me.

Then I phoned Heidi and told her I had bad news, but a solution to the bad news as well. She bloody loved the idea. Said it was even better than me simply single handing across. For me to limp over the finishing line against all the odds made great tele.

36 hours later, first thing in the morning the film crew picked me up for the first part of a long day's filming. The story was whilst I was waiting for the mechanic to turn up I was going to take a tourist trip on a horse drawn narrowboat.

Well, we got on this trip boat, it was the most boring thing to film and chat about with any animation, ever. However, being a boat bellend, I managed to make another great tit out of myself thinking they were going to turn the boat round for the return journey by winding it, as is usual. Except all they had to do was swop the horse with the tiller and vice versa for the return journey. That faux pas and me commenting on how lovely the horses arse was, was the sum total of me explaining to camera what a significant and historic method of transport I was enjoying.

Next up was me pretending I had finished my journey by visiting the very beginning of the Llangollen canal. This is where Thomas Telford built his weir in the early nineteenth century to redirect some of the River Dee to fill and maintain his newly built canal, the cameraman and I frantically googled.

This weir was known as Horseshoe Falls, was shaped as the name suggested, but wasn't really a fall as such, more of a 12 inch tumble. I couldn't resist taking the piss again. In fact they'd been filming me taking the piss from the get-go. I didn't go for the title Horseshoe Falls, instead I went for Welsh Niagra Falls…I think I was beginning to get hysterical. It was almost halfway through the day, I had to do a lot of tricky boat manoeuvring of which I was nowhere near and time was running away with itself.

CHAPTER 45

EUPHORIA TO HEARTBREAK

Everybody's Gotta Learn Sometime – Beck

Sail Away – David Gray

Wish You Were Here – Alpha Blondy

I got back to the boat shortly after lunch. The film crew were waiting for us half an hour's cruise away near the aqueduct.

Paul whose boat was facing the wrong way had to spend an hour turning it at the nearest winding hole to get in position to tow me.

It was then that the trouble began.

We hadn't thought about the technicalities of towing a boat. Boats don't have brakes and boats don't have steering when the engine is not running. Oh my god, it was like watching 2 people competing to make the biggest idiot out of themselves, ever.

We tied my front rope to the back of Pauls boat as you would with a car. Paul set off, my boat went sideways and crashed into the side of his boat. Paul set off again, got grounded and my little boat glided past him until the rope tightened and flicked the boat round crashing into Paul's and jamming the canal.

I take back everything I say about hire boaters and all I can say is I'm glad they weren't filming that bit.

We kept going in this vain until a lady boater approached us and said she'd been watching us whilst she was having lunch and decided to google how 2 people could possibly make bigger idiots out of themselves. Not really, just kidding, she googled how to tow a boat. Brilliant. Why didn't I think of that?

And that is how we learned to tow a boat properly and my god, what we were about to have to do next, we really did need to know how to tow a boat properly.

As I mentioned earlier, there's quite a carnival atmosphere on and around the Pontcysyllte aqueduct. The film crew had been busy filming general views so excitement was building with the tourists, or I should say the Gongoozlers as to what was about to occur.

Navigating this area is seriously tight. At one end there's a boat hire company and trip boats, at the other end all manner of floating markets. Mix that in with all the other boats queuing to cross the single width aqueduct plus the steady stream of people trying to walk along the narrow towpath of it and you've got a full blown traffic jam. Trying to film me being towed by a 60' boat, making us 90' long in total was going to be a bloody nightmare.

But, essentially good tele.

I was shitting it. We approached the tight right hand bend to get us into the basin where the boat company, trip boats and queued narrowboats were, swung the boats around and moored alongside a hire boat. Phew, managed that bit at least, or rather Paul did.

Because of continuity, it had to look like I'd broken down on the other side of the aqueduct. To film this, we obviously had to cross it, get to the winding hole on the other side untie the boats and turn them around. Obviously you can't turn a boat whilst towing, theres just not enough room or manoeuvrability. So this was crossing number 1.

I had to fake it again on camera pretending I'd just broken down and had thought of how I could resolve the problem and finish my adventure, by being towed across. Then I had to happen across Paul who had pulled his boat out of shot. It doesn't come easily this. I am dramatic, I'll give you that, but I'm no actress. Anyway, Sean the cameraman was happy with my fakery as I pretended I googled how to tow a boat. We then roped the boats together and set off to cross the Poncysyllte Aqueduct, one of the 7 wonders of the waterways, a UNESCO world heritage site and the end of my adventure.

The faking ramped up. Sean's filming on the back deck with me. James, the runner is filming hidden in a bush and Heidi the producer is filming from the narrow towpath. No pressure on me or my acting skills then.

Just before we set off for this, however, I poured myself a flask of medicinal cider. Just a quick note to make at this point, if you ever see me out on my boat and I have a flask in my hand, it may be tea, however the chances are it's cider...

Mercifully, the cider helped me not over think the situation and we crossed the aqueduct again, as if I had never set eyes on it before and it was an emotional limp to the finish line rather than a fall at the last hurdle. Thank fuck for cider, as I had to make all of this up! That was crossing number 2 that day.

Reaching the end of the crossing I was told we had to film the whole thing again, this time by drone. So that was us untying the boats, turning them around, retying them and returning once again across the aqueduct . Crossing number 3.

It was getting embarrassing this. As we passed the floating market traders for a second time, you could see people looking at us as if we were the biggest attention seeking drama queens known to man. The third time we passed, on the approach again to the aqueduct, they ignored us. Also, because there was no crew on board for this crossing it did indeed look like we were doing it for attention. Crossing number 4.

At the end of that cringeworthy crossing, we jumped off the boats for me to be filmed saying thanks to Paul, say I could relax now that my adventure was over and go to the pub. Which we duly did. The last bit of filming was of me sat in the beer garden enjoying (yet another) pint of cider. Just as well it was the last bit of filming, I was easily half cut by then.

We said a fond farewell to Heidi and the crew, got back to the boats, realised we had to be on the other side of the aqueduct for Big John who was back from his holidays and going to fix little boat the following day. That's us untying the boats, turning them around, retying and crossing that fucking aqueduct again. Crossing number 5. Fuck my days, at least the floating market traders had packed up.

We moored up ready for John the next day, beyond knackered and really quite shitfaced but extremely happy. We had had a great big long day mucking about with boats and cameras. What could have been better!

It was great to see John the next day, my knight in shining armour and a proper mechanic that could actually fix things.

It was whilst John was rebuilding the pump that had been reassembled backwards by Baby-Face, that the call came in.

The call was from Pete, Jel's partner. She had gone downhill, the disease was progressing faster than the meds were fighting it. They couldn't strip her immune system out and they couldn't put her in a coma. They were going to try a revolutionary new drug therapy using something called JAK inhibitors which blocked the pathways for the cells that were trying to eat each other, which was at the very core of the problem with this horrendous autoimmune disease she had.

Pete phoned on the Saturday and said they would begin this therapy that they had high hopes of when the specially commissioned drugs arrived, first thing Monday morning.

By the Monday morning though, Jel didn't need the drugs.

My best friend in all the world, my inspiration, my belly laugh and my conscience, died of the rare autoimmune disease known as Dermatomyositis on the Sunday.

And the world stopped spinning.

EPILOGUE

There was no need for me to rush anywhere. No need for me to do anything. No distractions. After breaking the distressing news to my kids, I curled into a ball.

Although Jel and I were as close as sisters, I was not family. There was no family huddle, no discussion of procedures, no heartfelt conversations.

My grief was nothing compared to her family's grief. Who was I to pile my grief on top of theirs? It was time to take a step back, give them space to mourn her.

Which compounded it. Made me curl into an even tighter ball.

After a few days, Jules and I both realised we needed the support of each other, so she came and stayed on the boat with me, on that bewitching Welsh canal that had a gentle flow coming from the river feeding it, a soothing lull to the ache we had in our hearts.

Another few days later and I was at the airport waiting for my daughter Kitty, who had been away travelling to arrive home. She had been in tatters too, had known Jel, her Godmother all her life. She had been a great Godmother. Jelly used to sit there for hours picking Kitty's spots! I know, disgusting, isn't it? Everything becomes endearing in loss though, it seems.

To have Kitty home soothed both our souls. It had been like having a limb missing whilst she was away and we now clung to each other desperately, trying to squeeze the love in and the heartbreak away.

This was the period of mourning after death and before funeral, where decisions are agreed on, choices selected, procedures followed. None of them I had any business helping with, although I desperately wanted to. Instead I cooked food, and delivered it. Checking on the family as I did so. But they had lots of food. There was no room for my help.

The funeral came. It was the most heartbreaking day of my life. There were hundreds and hundreds of mourners, I saw few however. I huddled with my children, family and closest friends. This was not a time to be social. I can't think about it now without crying. Tears are simply rolling out of me whilst writing this.

After the service and walking away, touching her coffin, knowing she was inside and I would never see her again, tore my heart to shreds.

After the funeral it felt like we were all seeds in a dandelion clock that had been blown in separate directions by grief. The pain was too much to handle to be near to each other. Too harsh a reminder of her death.

Kitty and I chose the boat as our source of respite. And she was indeed that.

The place of solace and healing, distraction and happiness. The fact that Kitty felt it too made me love that little boat even more, if that were possible.

This little boat, purchased on a whim with a small budget, has grown mightier in my heart and soul than anything I could imagine. The toil and torture of restoring her and refitting her. The profound financial gamble and upheaval in lifestyle to afford this gamble. All is forgotten. She has thrown trials of such magnitude at me, made me stronger in both mind and body. Given me sanctuary, solace and comfort. She has given me such exploits as to appease the adventure seeking risk taker in me.

But above all, this little boat has healed me. The gap in my heart has mended. The loneliness banished.

I play a song every day that reminds me of Jelly, my beautiful, inspiring best friend in all the world. Kitty plays it every day too, from her home now in Melbourne Australia.

The three of us loved listening to it every time we set off for another adventure on The Dawn Piper.

It's 'For The Summer' by Ray LaMontagne and the Pariah Dogs.

It's customary to write 'The End' once finishing writing a book. However, this is not the end. My adventures with The Dawn Piper have extended far and continue to do so. Magazine articles, interviews and of course the tele. Jelly would have loved watching me on the tele. Well, mostly she would have loved taking the piss out of me on the tele.

In memory of Christine Cummings 31-01–1969 to 21-05-2023

Printed in Dunstable, United Kingdom